Predicative Minds

Predicative Minds

The Social Ontogeny of Propositional Thinking

Radu J. Bogdan

A Bradford Book

The MIT Press
Cambridge, Massachusetts
London, England

For information about special quantity discounts, please email <special_sales@mitpress.mit.edu>.

This book was set in Stone Sans and Stone Serif by SNP Best-set Typesetter Ltd., Hong Kong.

Printed and bound in the United States of America.

Library of Congress Cataloging-in-Publication Data

Bogdan, Radu J.
Predicative minds: the social ontogeny of propositional thinking / Radu J. Bogdan.
p. cm.
Includes bibliographical references and index.
ISBN 978-0-262-02636-9 (hardcover : alk. paper)
1. Thought and thinking—Social aspects. 2. Thought and thinking. 3. Philosophy of mind. I. Title.
BF441.B625 2009
153.4'3—dc22

2008032751

10 9 8 7 6 5 4 3 2 1

To the memory of my uncle, my very dear Tache; and to all those good people who cared

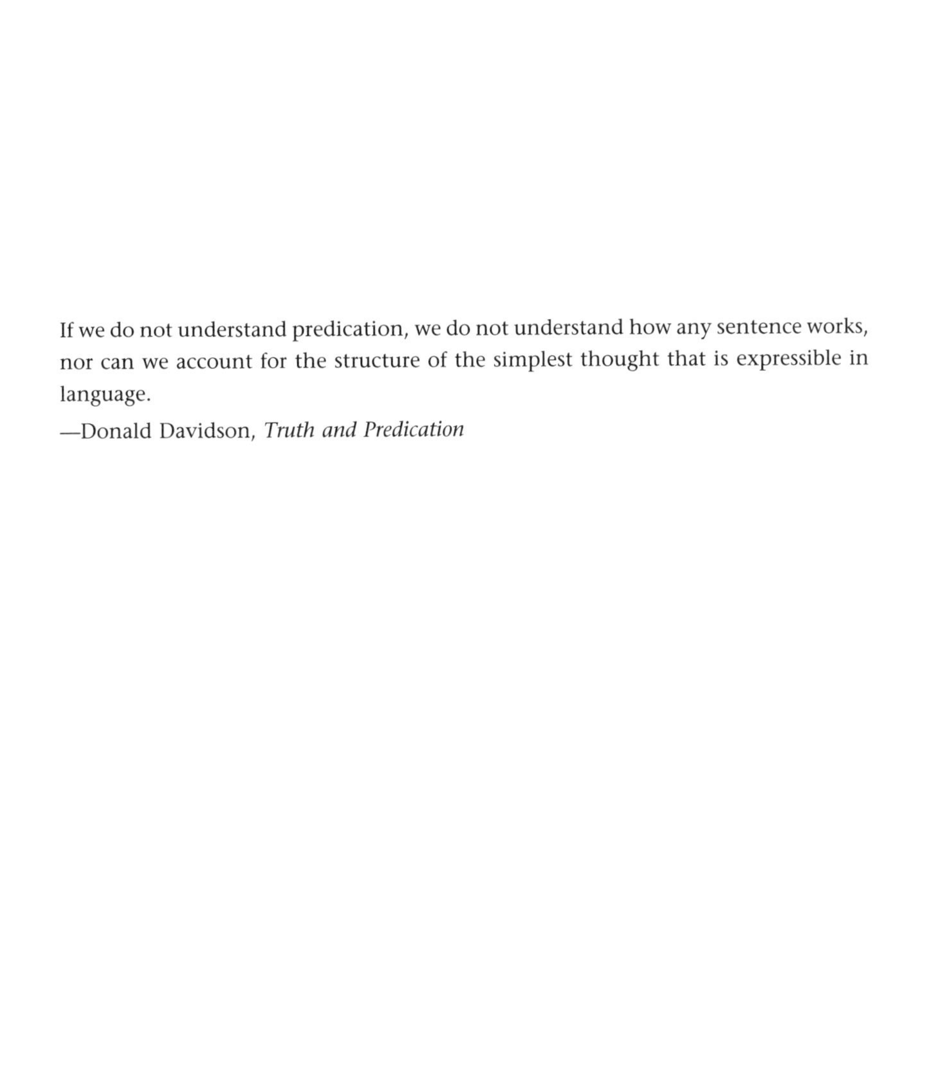

If we do not understand predication, we do not understand how any sentence works, nor can we account for the structure of the simplest thought that is expressible in language.

—Donald Davidson, *Truth and Predication*

Contents

Preface

About fifteen years ago, I joined a growing group of psychologists and a few philosophers in the realization that naive psychology (or theory of mind) is a basic mental competence that evolved to represent and make sense of other minds and our own. That realization eventually went into a book (Bogdan 1997). Work on that book brought the further realization, shared by a much smaller group of developmental psychologists, that naive psychology is also a mind designer, as it enables, often generates, and even shapes a host of other mental faculties, and in particular reflexive thinking or thinking about our own thoughts. This new realization, too, went into a book (Bogdan 2000). This book continues the mind-design theme of the second book, actually a variation of it, as it explores the predicative roots of human thinking.

Predication is construed here as a mental competence—apparently uniquely human—that is exercised intently when one attributes explicitly a property to an object, an action to an agent, a relation to two or more objects, and so on. As far as I can tell, predication is a rather surprising competence, in philosophical, psychological, and evolutionary terms. It cannot be explained by just having and applying concepts, possessing a language, with its grammar, semantics, and pragmatics, or exercising other mental faculties, such as learning, attention, or perception. The capacity to predicate appears to be neither innate nor learned, yet it is universal among humans. And somehow, predication manages to produce thoughts and sentences that are more than the sum of their parts. Puzzling in its properties and history, the mental competence for predication still awaits a coherent and plausible explanation. This book takes up the challenge by inquiring into its developmental origins and raison d'être.

Although not a psychologist, I find that development—more than intuitions or conceptual analysis, the usual tools of the philosopher, or the abstract and functional boxes-and-arrows models of the cognitive scientist—provides a most useful and systematic angle from which to figure out the design of the human mind in general and the predicative design of human thinking in particular. Predication, it turns out, is not only an outcome of development, as everything in an organism is, but also and essentially a by-product of uniquely human features of development, some of them quite unrelated to representation, cognition, and thinking. This truth, I think, would not have become apparent without a close look at development. If the human mind is unique, it is because human mental development is unique. The development of the competence for predication reflects this uniqueness by drawing on and blending several disparate and equally remarkable abilities, also explored in some detail here, such as intersubjective coregulation, communicating meanings, representing reference, and acquiring words. This developmental cocktail opens an unequaled window on the early design of the human mind.

The writing of this book overlapped with an unexpected and dramatic period in Catalina's and my life (and that of so many other people), during which the solidarity, warmth, and support of many friends (and also good-hearted strangers) enabled us to carry on with our life and work, almost normally. In the order of our peregrinations, our heartfelt thanks go to Jeannie and Richard Lee (in Fayetteville, Arkansas), Adrienne and Keith Lehrer as well as David Schmidtz (in Tucson, Arizona), and Barbara Moely and Harvey Green (on return in New Orleans). From a distance but as close in spirit and friendship, the constantly warm and supportive Helen Seidler and Owen Mitz, Alice ter Meulen, Luca Mezincescu, Gina and Sorel Vieru, and my sister Adriana watched over our well-being and helped in all sorts of ways, earning our warm gratitude. During this turbulent period, I lost my dear uncle, a second father to me. I miss him very much. I dedicate this book to his memory and to all these good people, who cared deeply when it mattered.

Many other people, in different places, deserve our thanks for their sensitivity and help. I am thinking in particular of those good souls in Tucson who did their best to make us feel at home for a few months—in particular, Lilian Jacques and John Pollock, Chris Maloney, and Massimo Piatelli-Palmarini (whose sonorous and melodic name I always wanted to appropriate, with no success so far).

On a professional level, I want to thank those who read or heard and commented on fragments and ideas of this book—especially Keith Lehrer and David Olson, anonymous reviewers of the manuscript, and audiences at the University of Arizona, the University of Bucharest (and Mircea

Dumitru and Sorin Vieru in particular), the Institut Jean Nicod in Paris (and Pierre Jacob in particular), and in Turkey, Bilkent University, the Middle Eastern Technical University (both in Ankara), Bogazici University (and Ilhan Inan in particular), and Koc University (both in Istanbul).

I want also to thank the MIT Press team for a very fine job at each stage in the development of this book: senior editor Tom Stone, for his constant interest in and support of the project, copyeditor Cindy Milstein for carefully dotting the right i's throughout the manuscript, and production editor Deborah Cantor-Adams for helpfully and graciously putting all the pieces together.

During the final writing of this book, Bilkent University and my colleagues in philosophy and psychology provided a congenial, stimulating, and pleasant place to live and work, for which Catalina and I are grateful. *Tesekkür ederim!*

Introduction

When conscious and explicit, human thoughts have a number of singular properties. One of them is being predicative. In a predicative mode, one can think and say of a house that it is big, a car that it is to the left of the house, a cat that it is about to jump, a hypothesis that it is plausible, this book that it is worth reading, or the like. The idea, in this formulation, is that a predicative mind singles out and represents an item (thing, agent, event, situation, and so on) in order to attribute to it—or to direct at it, as I prefer to put it—the representation of another item (be it property, relation, action, evaluation, and so forth).

Puzzling Thoughts

The mental practice of predication may not look like big deal, but I think it is. It is an immensely big deal and quite puzzling too, in evolutionary, psychological, and philosophical terms. Predication is *evolutionarily* puzzling because it is not practiced by other animal minds—at least not according to the analysis proposed here. Predication is *developmentally* puzzling because the thoughts of young children begin like those of other animals, operating in imperative and nonpredicative forms, yet when they turn descriptive and predicative, around the age of two or so, the transition looks less like a gradual maturation from simpler precursors and more like a rather revolutionary change. Finally, predication is *philosophically* puzzling, for several reasons. The oldest and best-known reason is that a predication is more than the sum of its parts. The thought that the lawn is green represents more then the parts—lawn, green, is—represent separately, as a conjunction or mere list. Another reason why predication is philosophically or (perhaps better said) cognitive-scientifically puzzling is that it is not reducible to, and hence cannot be explained by, its conceptual, logical, grammatical, semantic, and even pragmatic properties, as was and still is assumed by most theorists of predication. Or so I will argue.

Predication marks a sharp divide between animal and human minds, and between the minds of young children and those of older children and adults. Predication is also at the heart of conscious, deliberate, explicit, and language-based human thinking. Predicative thoughts are the fuel of higher mental activities, such as deliberation, reflective planning, hypothetical reasoning, introspection, counterfactual imagination, theorizing, reflective self-control, and more. Predicative minds are the only ones that create art, technology, culture, and science. So many reasons, then, to ask the question—the central question of this book: what explains predication as a mental competence?

Many Faces

Predication is a multifaceted phenomenon. It operates as a mental representation, which can also take a linguistic form—hence as a thought and sentence, respectively—and is thus the output of a family of mental acts produced by the exercise of a mental competence. To understand the competence, it is important to approach its manifest outputs from the right angle, with the right notions. To this end, chapter 1 begins with a distinction between two sets of dimensions that characterize predicative outputs and therefore the mental acts that generate them. One set contains the standard dimensions, to be called *S-dimensions*, such as language, formal structure, concepts, and truth conditions. The other set contains less visible but as important dimensions, to be called *P-dimensions*, such as predicate-to-subject directedness, topic-comment-presupposition format, and intended descriptiveness. This distinction suggests a parallel one about propositions as contents of thoughts. A predicative proposition, I will argue, is one that satisfies both sets of dimensions, whereas a proposition that has only the standard S-dimensions represents only (what I will call) a *coinstantiation* of an object and a property, an agent and an action, or the like. To understand the difference between coinstantiation and predication is to understand the essential contribution of the P-dimensions to the acts of predication. This is also the difference between the approach taken in this book and most other accounts of predication.

Different Answers about Coinstantiation

Chapter 2 turns to some major accounts of predication that aim to explain predication, but as far as I can see, end up explaining only coinstantiation.

First examined are classical accounts and in particular Gottlob Frege's—notorious for its indifference to psychology and yet influential beyond philosophy. The chapter then looks at several psychologically sensitive accounts of predication. One account, shared by many philosophers and linguists, insists on predication being inherent in the syntactic formalism of a language, whether mental or natural. Another account derives the predicative format of animal thoughts from possessing and joining the concepts of objects, properties, relations, and so on. A third account finds the roots of predicative propositions in the naive psychology that interprets other minds. A fourth holds that the predicative format of thinking and communication is inherent in how visual perception works. Still another and somewhat related psychological account is that the predicative format is inherent in how attention works. Finally, a pragmatic account focuses on one central P-dimension (the topic-comment format), but ignores the others and stops short of exploring the mental underpinnings of predication. There are other versions as well, but the ones explored in chapter 2 are among the most influential and plausible. As far as I can see, none really explains the mental competence for predication, and most are about coinstantiation. Predication is thus in need of a different explanation, concerned primarily with its three most critical P-dimensions, the ones that really make the difference.

The Hypothesis

If I were to place my hypothesis in a philosophical lineage, I would note that David Hume and Immanuel Kant may have been the first major philosophers to treat the problem of predication under a psychologically relevant angle, in terms of how the mind works. Reacting to Hume's skepticism about how the mind unites distinct representations (i.e., only through coinstantiation by association, in my terms), Kant posited spontaneously active and purposeful judgments as mental unifiers, and in particular as acts of predication. Donald Davidson notes that unlike Hume, Kant was not aware that he had not addressed, let alone solved, the problem of the unity of predication. The unity problem, according to Davidson (2005, 99), is to explain what the mind adds to the components of a predication—e.g., lawn, green, is—to produce the predicative judgment that the lawn is green. Nevertheless, I think that Kant had the right insight: predication *is* a mental construction, a spontaneously active and purposeful judgment, made possible by certain abilities of the human mind. The unity itself, I will contend in chapter 3, results from how the P-dimensions, reflecting these abilities, animate and organize predicative judgments. The psychological question, then, is what mental abilities are responsible for this accomplishment.

My hypothesis is that these P-abilities (as I will call them) are assembled gradually and cumulatively out of developments originating in disparate faculties that operate in disparate domains, for a variety of reasons that are initially unrelated to predication. These faculties constitute the main roots of predication, according to chapter 4. The first root is the adult-infant physiological coregulation, which later takes a psychological turn as bilateral and intersubjective communication by shared meaning. A second root is the young child's imperative and world-bound communication that treats adults as a means to the child's goals. A third root is the child's development of a sense of other minds, which builds mostly on the bilateral mental sharing of infancy and later on a growing naive psychology (or theory of mind).

The contribution of these roots to predication takes the form of an *ontogenetic staircase* leading successively to the child's sense of communicative meaning, prelinguistic coreference, and finally word coreference introduced by the adult's explicit acts of naming in contexts of shared attention. The child's mental scheme of explicit and shared word coreference becomes the source and template for the child's earliest predicative judgments.

The developmental process that generates this ontogenetic staircase is, according to chapter 5, one of *assembly*—as opposed to either maturation out of an innate base dedicated to predication, or learning by association and imitation. On this assembly view, distinct abilities and dispositions are recruited, joined, and blended together by successive challenges—some of them adult inspired or guided—that the young child's mind encounters and must handle adaptively, as it advances on the ontogenetic staircase to shared attention, then word acquisition, and finally predication.

Although chapter 5 concludes the developmental story of predication, it is worth meditating on its possible historical and neuropsychological implications, which is the topic of chapter 6. Since the abilities and dispositions that contribute to predication originate in separate faculties operating in separate domains (the roots of predication), and have initial functions unrelated to predication, it looks like the competence for predication may have first evolved as an *incidental* effect of selection for more basic ontogenetic adaptations for interpersonal coregulation, communication, language acquisition, and the assimilation of culture. The selection in question may have at first been mostly sexual and conducive to a revolution in parenting, probably rather recent historically. This parental revolution would explain the intense and intricate communicational interactions between children and adults, and the escalating arms race during which new mental acquisitions of the child are met with new challenges, mostly linguistic and cultural, initiated by adults. The responses of the young minds may have begun as improvisations, whose successful versions may have ended up genetically assimilated as ontogenetic adaptations.

In a nutshell, then, this book maintains that humans develop predicative minds for several disparate reasons, mostly noncognitive, which bear initially on physiological coregulation, affective and manipulative communication, and the acquisition of words. Once developed, the competence for predication in turn redesigns human thinking and linguistic communication. This is why understanding the uniqueness and representational power of the human mind requires an explanation of why and how predication came to be. This book proposes such an explanation.

Credits

The search for an explanation took my inquiry into quite disparate territories—from the philosophy of mind and language to psycholinguistics and developmental psychology—that is, wherever I thought the empirical evidence was relevant and the theoretical insights useful. Along the way, at critical junctures, the search had some good guides. Thus, it was helped considerably by the bright and illuminating signposts first planted by Lev Vygotsky and his school several decades ago, which revealed some essential psychosocial contours of the human mind. These signposts were later rearranged more tightly, around the narrower area of the child's intersubjective communication, naive psychology, and language acquisition, by a cluster of broad-minded interdisciplinary developmentalists, ranging from Jerome Bruner to Peter Hobson and Michael Tomasello. But the ontogeny of predication being what I think it is—a mosaic of interacting ontogenetic adaptations—the search also took my inquiry into the territory of the child's (mostly) imperative communication, which was superbly mapped by Elizabeth Bates, working mostly with the tools of the alternative Piagetian tradition. Equally insightful was David Olson's pioneering analysis of the ontogenesis of propositions. Martha Gibson's survey of philosophical theories of predication was a useful guide to a large, complicated, but alas psychologically unilluminating literature. Other debts will of course be credited in the text. But the ones just cited deserve early recognition, as they paved the way to my understanding of the mental side of predication.

I The Territory

1 The Many Faces of Predication

This chapter maps the territory to be covered in this book. Section 1.1 begins with a conceptual portrait of predication drawn along two sets of dimensions, which I call *list S* and *list P*. The list S contains such standard dimensions as language, its expressions, and their formal structure, concepts, and truth conditions, among others, whereas the list P contains less visible but as important, if not more important, mental and pragmatic dimensions, such as predicate-to-subject directedness, topic-comment-presupposition format, and intended descriptiveness. Section 1.2 suggests that as the content of a thought, a predicative proposition is one that meets the conditions on both lists S and P. An S-dimensioned proposition is only minimal and nonpredicative. According to section 1.3, if the content of a thought is only S-dimensioned, so to speak, it merely joins the representation of an object to that of a property, an agent to that of an action, and so on. This is coinstantiation, as I will call it, but not predication. The notion of coinstantiation will be the main critical weapon used against a variety of accounts of predication.

1.1 Dimensions of Predication

Predications are the bread and butter of human propositional thinking and language use. When I think or judge, and say, that this pig is fat, I predicate—mentally and linguistically—a property (fatness) of an individual (this pig). I could have also predicated a relation of two (or more) individuals, as when I think and say, for example, that this pig is fatter than the one over there, or that this pig is the same as the one I saw yesterday. If I think that [the large and beautiful tree is to the left of the car], I predicate a relation (to the left) of two items of variable complexity (the large and beautiful tree, the car). The predicative mind also treats identity, analogy, or comparison as relations, hence predications, in largely similar terms.

Most of our predicative thoughts are of these sorts—object-property, agent-action, and various kinds of relations between two or among three or more items. Most of our deliberate and conscious thoughts are predicative, although not as simplistic as these examples may suggest. Predication, in short, is a way of linking concepts in a thought or judgment, expressed propositionally in an utterance or written sentence, to the effect that certain arrangements obtain among the items that the thought or judgment represents. This formulation is almost right but not quite, as we shall see. But it will do for the moment.

We can look at predication from (at least) three distinct angles. One angle is that of the *output*, the resulting representation, whether in the form of a judgment or utterance. I will treat the notions of judgment and thought as equivalently about the occurrent representational output of some mental act, and leave the notion of proposition to characterize the content of a thought or judgment. Another angle on predication is that of the *mental act* of predicating—or rather the activity, because it is a fairly complex set of acts—that produces the output representation. And a third angle is that of the *mental competence* whose exercise results in predicative acts. The aim of this book is to understand this competence, what it is, and where it comes from—to understand, in other words, what it takes to become a predicative mind and operate like one. But understanding the competence depends on getting the right story of the outputs, the predications, because it is through the latter that the competence is manifested and thus approachable theoretically. So the first task is to have a clear idea of what predication is. Given the examples just given, a sensible suggestion seems to be that a predication is a union or joining of two or more mental and/or linguistic representations that satisfy certain conditions. Commonsense reflection joins a philosophical and psychological consensus that a predicative judgment or thought, linguistically expressed, must at least have the following features or dimensions.

The S-List

A predicative judgment or thought

- represents information in some *code* or language [encoding]
- its information is *categorized* under some recognition devices, from sensory discriminations to *thematic* categories and concepts that represent objects, properties, agents, actions, etc. [thematic categorization]
- is *structured* by some combinatorial capacity into distinct components [linkage]

- reflects structurally thematic relations, such as object-property, agent-action, or object-relation-object [thematic structure]
- there are items, facts, and situations in the world that the thought is *about* and *true* of [aboutness and truth conditions]

I call these the *S-dimensions*. For exegetical reasons, the wording of the first dimension, concerning encoding, is left vague to allow for the possibility (later denied) of nonlinguistic animal or infant predication. Likewise, the wording of the linkage dimension is left vague to allow for the possibility of nongrammatical combinations in animal or infantile thinking. For the purposes of our discussion, the difference between categories and concepts is that the latter alone are embedded in complex networks that allow logical transitions and inferences. A dog surely has the category of cat (full stop), but may fail to connect it to the related categories of animal, mammal, feline, bird hunter, and so on, in which case the dog is a categorizer but not a conceptualizer.

The list S reflects (what we may call) a *structural perspective* on predication. It is the *standard* perspective on predication. It is also a perspective that reveals the *surface* form of predication. (Three good reasons for the S prefix.) According to the list S, predication is manifested and visible in its symbolic expression, grammatical organization, logical form, the concepts employed, and the resulting semantic content as propositional meaning.

The S-dimensions are clearly necessary for predication. But are they also *sufficient*? If they were, as the sole guide to predication, then the competence for predication would consist basically of the language resources, whether mental or natural, thematic categories or concepts, and some combinatorial or general reasoning abilities. The acts of predication would then amount to recognizing and categorizing inputs along thematic lines (objects, properties, etc.), and linking the thematic categorizations in (what I will call) minimally propositional coinstantiations. It turns out, as noted in the next chapter, that most theories of predication—in philosophy, linguistics, and psychology—take the list S to be definitive of predication, thus adopting the structural perspective, and differ only over which S-resources are involved and at what level of cognitive complexity.

What else is there, one may reasonably ask? After all, an S-dimensioned output does seem to be all there is to predication as a form of representing information; and the mental acts that produce the output, by exercising the underlying faculties, seem all that is required psychologically to have a predicative mind. *Seem* is, indeed, the right word, and *representing* not quite the right one. On the analysis proposed here, the S-dimensions, and the mental acts and faculties they reveal, are only the tip of an iceberg. Most of the predication iceberg is under the S-surface, so to speak, and not visible without the right theoretical eyes. When, with the right eyes, we peek below the surface, we realize that predication is not just a representational enterprise and certainly has not initially developed as one. To see why, consider the strikingly parallel—and indeed quite related—story of propositional meaning.

The Meaning Parallel

There are different accounts of propositional meaning. Until recently, most focused on the sentence and regarded its propositional meaning in terms close to the S-dimensions such as truth conditions, what its concepts represent, the inferential role of the sentence, the larger contextual conditions in which the sentence can be asserted or its truth established, or so on. Simplifying somewhat but not too much, these structural accounts can be said to analyze propositional meaning in terms of what it takes for a sentence (or some other sort of symbolic expression) to *represent* what it does. This is the semantic notion of meaning as representation.

This structural perspective on propositional meaning has been challenged by a pragmatic perspective, adopted by a variety of accounts, most of them tied to communication and the use of ordinary language. The one of interest here is what may be called the *psychopragmatic* account of communicative meaning, anticipated by George Mead (1910, 1934) and elaborated analytically by Paul Grice (1957). Grice replaces the sentence with the (token) *utterance* as a basic unit of analysis, and the sentential meaning with the speaker's intended meaning that is directed at an audience on a particular occasion. As a result, the meaning of a sentence results from what its speaker intently means by uttering it. For Grice, then, sentential meaning derives from the mental act of the speaker, which is the act of meaning something on a particular occasion. And the act of meaning itself expresses the intent to convey information by producing a mental effect in an audience. There will be more on this Gricean story and its implications for predication in chapter 4, section 4.1.

Important to note right now is the fact that the Gricean account switches the frame of analysis of propositional meaning from the formal and conceptual structure and the semantics of a *sentence* (as a visible and frozen output, so to speak) to the psychology of the mental act of *intending* to communicate through a particular *utterance*. It is a switch from meaning as representation to meaning as intent to use information with a social effect. I will propose a rather similar switch in the analysis of predication, from the set of representation-bound structural and semantic S-dimensions to a set of dimensions that reflect the unique psychopragmatic design of *predicating*. I call them the P-dimensions. They go beyond semantic representation, and reflect mental intent and, at least in early development, its social impact.

The P-List

According to the new list, a predicative thought also

- intently and *explicitly directs* the content of a thematic representation or more at the referent of another thematic representation or more, thus instantiating a thematic relation, such as object-property, agent-action, or agent-relation-object [intended directedness]
- organizes the resulting content in a specific, limited, and well-structured *topic-comment-presupposition format*, and makes this content, so organized, available to further predicatively sensitive mental operations [topic-comment-presupposition format]
- and does so in an intently *descriptive*, reportorial, or declarative manner [intended descriptiveness]

Suppose I think that [this house is big]. This thought emerges out of the exercise of a mental competence that selects and directs the representation of a property (bigness) at the representation of an object (house), and in so doing, describes or states a fact. According to the analysis of the next few chapters, the predicative nexus between property and object (or other thematic patterns of predication) is not just joining them in some pattern. The notion of intended directedness is meant to identify an additional factor that is involved in the predicative nexus. What the predicate represents (e.g., a property) is mentally directed, intendingly, at what the subject term refers to (e.g., an object), even though this intended directedness may no longer be apparent in most routine predications.

This first P-dimension reflects the mental activism of predications (so to speak)—that is, the fact that the predicator has initiative and control over what and how they represent propositionally. A mere coinstantiation of thematic categories, triggered by some perceptual or memory input, usually is passive and reflex, as in general is nonpredicative thinking. Mutatis mutandis, this difference is echoed in that between Grice's speaker's meaning and the standard representational meaning of a sentence.

Another factor, also responsible for the specificity and unity of predication, is identified in the next dimension. Unless it emerges out of the blue, in a sort of "mental ballistics" (to use a metaphor of Galen Strawson), a predicative thought normally occurs within a presuppositional envelope, whose main elements are: a broader theme or context, as part of a train of thought, discourse, or conversation; some background information; some expectations; and some goal, as part of a well-aimed "mental artillery." Within this envelope, a predicative judgment has a specific topic, which it focuses on (the house, in our earlier example), and makes a comment about it (that it is big). Although in this example and many others the grammatical subject is the topic and the grammatical predicate is the comment, the topic-comment tandem can be extremely flexible, often transcending the narrow distinction between grammatical subject and predicate.

Finally, a predication is (again) intendingly or deliberately descriptive or reportorial, as it aims to state, describe, or inform about a definite and limited fact or situation. Moreover, it does so in terms that are publicly intelligible or shared, as opposed to egocentric or self-centered. This dimension may look trivial but it is not. Like the other two P-dimensions, it is not implicit in and cannot be derived solely from the S-dimensions. As argued later, an intended descriptiveness is not inherent in just having thoughts, nor is it inherent in such thoughts just being propositional.

Two-Tiered Operation

This way of looking at predication anticipates a two-tiered operation of the predication competence. To put it somewhat metaphorically, we may say that the mental abilities responsible for the P-dimensions—P-abilities, as I call them—form the hidden and underground core of predication, whereas the S-abilities form its outer and visible shell. The mental acts of predication can be said to convert the work of the P-abilities into the work of the S-abilities, thus mapping the deeper psychopragmatic P-dimensions onto the surface expressive, conceptual, and formal (logical and grammatical) S-dimensions. So construed, the predication competence can be said to operate at two levels: the P-level first, and then the S-level.

The proposal, elaborated in later chapters, is that the predicator *begins* by intending to direct the meaning of a predicate word at the referent of a subject word, as a comment about a topic, in order to share or convey descriptively some information (level P), which is then represented according to the S-dimensions (level S). The intentful act of directing is the *mental* (or psycho) component of predicating. The *pragmatic* component reflects the context-dependent topic-comment-presupposition matrix underlying a predication. So construed, predicating amounts to a set of psychopragmatic acts whose output is encapsulated in an explicit representation with propositional content. Neither the mental nor the pragmatic components of a predication are necessarily manifest in the output structure that normally reflects only the surface S-dimensions—whence the tempting illusion of predication as mere representation.

For both the producer and consumer of predications, activating or tracking (respectively) the P-dimensions of predication requires *going beyond the output or surface representation* that embodies only the S-dimensions. For the producer, it is a matter of thinking or judging predicatively, according to the P-dimensions; for the consumer, it is a matter of inferring the P-dimensions from the context, other clues, and what is literally said in terms of S-dimensions. This is how communication works in general (Sperber and Wilson 1986). As in the parallel case of the Gricean notion of meaning, the communication angle is crucial, if we want to understand the origins of and reasons for predication.

Think, for a moment, of the alternative angle. If human thinking were built solely around a competence to represent the world, as widely assumed in philosophy and cognitive science, then it could do the job just fine with the mental faculties, acts, and structures that reflect the S-dimensions—hence nonpredicatively. This will be the critical point about coinstantiation in the next chapter: it could well do the job of representation, without predication. This contrast begins to suggest that predication might not originate in the representational resources of the mind, and might not have evolved for reasons having primarily to do with success in representation. Indeed, I will argue, although it ends up as the inextricable core of human thinking, predication actually enters the house of thinking, in early childhood, not through the front door of mental representation, but rather through the back doors (there are several) of interpersonal coregulation, intersubjective interactions, and the intent to influence other minds, all converging on word acquisition as the antechamber of predication.

1.2 Two Kinds of Propositions

For both the critical and constructive side of my argument, the distinction between the S- and P-dimensions needs to be related to, and further refined in terms of, other notions that are technically associated with predication. I begin with the controversial notion of proposition, modestly intended here to characterize the content of a representation, whether mental, linguistic, or logical.

Suppose I say, "This guy is not nice," and you ask, "What do you mean?" You fully understand the literal meaning of what I said. That literal meaning is what I will call a *minimal proposition*. I call it "minimal" in order to contrast it with a predicative proposition. A minimal proposition can be the semantic content of a list, such as <this, guy, not nice>, conjunction <this&guy¬ nice>, an abstract formula, as in the predicate calculus, on which more anon, or psychologically, of a thought that has a specific combinatorial pattern, with its own unity, which is *not* predicative. In the case of the list, conjunction, or the abstract formula, I would say that the content is a *logically* minimal proposition, and in the case of the (nonpredicative) thought a *psychologically* minimal proposition.

Your question was about what *I meant* to say—that is, what *I intended* to convey, informationally and attitudinally, by saying what I did. It may be that the guy was the topic of some prior conversation, in a context where being nice or not mattered. My predication projects the literal meaning of what I said, and hence the logically minimal proposition expressed, onto this psychopragmatic background. The intended result is a *predicative proposition*—that is, one that also satisfies the P-dimensions. A thought, therefore, is predicatively propositional only when, and thus because, it is intended to represent some state of affairs according to the P-dimensions.

According to later chapters, an animal or infant thought has only a *psychologically* minimal proposition as content. Such kinds of thoughts are mental vehicles (though not necessarily sentences in a natural language or symbol structures in a mental language) that represent various kinds of items, according to the S-dimensions, and therefore have truth-values in virtue of what they represent in some combinatorial pattern. As noted in the next section, this combinatorial pattern has its own sort of functional unity, but one that is not predicative.

The Unit Question

One may ask why two notions of proposition are needed to characterize psychologically the contents of thoughts—that is, one minimal (list S) and one predicative (lists S and P). Why not a single, standard notion of S-proposition as the predicative content of thoughts, leaving inference and context to fill in the P-dimensions? This is a fair and reasonable question. My preference for two notions is motivated by two related reasons. First, I do not think that minds, whether animal or human, think and communicate just by having semantic contents—that is, by representing, literally, in terms of minimal propositions. Such contents are likely to be cognitively and behaviorally inert, unless inserted in wider dynamic ensembles that reflect psychopragmatic parameters, such as those on the P-list in the human case (Bogdan 1989). In that case, the *unit* of thinking and communication is bound to be a psychopragmatic rather than merely semantic content. If a predicative thought or utterance is such a deliberately formed unit, then it must reflect more than its S-core of representation as semantic content.

Second, and relatedly, there is the tough problem of the "unity of the proposition" (the fact that as a content of thought, a predicative proposition is more than the sum of its parts). The unity is assumed to define the nature of predication. Mighty minds, from Plato and Aristotle to Frege, Bertrand Russell, Ludwig Wittgenstein, Willard Van Orman Quine, and Peter Strawson, among others, have struggled with this problem, apparently without much success (for recent surveys and evaluations, see Davidson 2005; Gibson 2004). Their attempted solutions in general focused on the logically minimal propositions as the contents of predicative thoughts. Yet again, these contents are cognitively inert, and no different from the list or sum of their parts. Indeed, these contents are inert *because* they lack unity.

It stands to reason, then, that what secures the unity of predication also demarcates the *unit* of predication. By lacking unity, a list or sum of elements cannot be a unit of predication. Nor can a minimal proposition, either logically or psychologically. The unity and therefore the unit of predication are in the eyes of the beholder, so to speak—that is, of the one who predicates or understands a predication. And the eyes of the beholder, as predicator, see not only the S-dimensions but also, and essentially, the P-dimensions. Seeing only the S-dimensions, as necessary and sufficient for predication, leads to a different, popular, yet misguided notion, already anticipated but further elaborated next.

1.3 Coinstantiation

The distinctions introduced in this chapter—between S-dimensions and P-dimensions, and correlatively, between minimal and predicative propositions as the contents of thoughts—provide the main critical tool that will be employed, mostly in the next chapter but also later, against alternative accounts of predication.

The basic idea is simple. It is that representations that possess only the S-dimensions are *coinstantiations*. A coinstantiative representation is one that joins or links thematic representations in some combinatorial but *nonpredicative* pattern. The content of a coinstantiative representation may be propositional minimally, and hence truth-valuable, without being predicative. Given the earlier distinction between logically and psychologically minimal propositions, we can distinguish between *logical* and *mental* coinstantiations. Both are nonpredicative, but the logical coinstantiation, unlike the mental one, is an abstract representation that satisfies the S-dimensions only and makes no assumption about the mental pattern in which thematic categories are linked, and hence has no unity. (Think of the difference as that between the notion of a circle defined in geometry and the representation of a physical circle.) A mental coinstantiation satisfies the S-dimensions in mental terms, which confer a psychologically coinstantiative unity to it.

A logical coinstantiation is a unit only by stipulation, not intrinsically. Consider the predicate calculus. A logician or mathematician may translate the logical or set-theoretical formula "Cx" in ordinary language as "x is C" without actually predicating C of x, but rather indicating the co-occurrence of a property and a variable, or the exemplification of the concept C by a class of entities subsumed under the variable x. This example suggests that even when the copula is treated as a "truth rule" that establishes when a sentence is true—namely, when the predicate term is true of the referent of the subject term (Wiggins 1984)—it does not follow that the sentence is actually predicative and that the "is" in question is of predication. On my analysis, as a truth rule, this "is" (as in "x is C") is an "is" of logical coinstantiation. One might suggest that logical coinstantiation is actually *logical* predication. I have no quarrel with the words employed, only with the concepts assumed. The point is that such "logical predication" has little in common with mental predication in thinking or linguistic predication in communication.

In contrast, mental coinstantiations normally result from the concomitant or successive application, through innate programs or acquired habits, of thematic categories, in a spontaneous, usually automatic or reflex manner, without reflection, deliberation, or intent. Spontaneous perceptual or memory judgments that lead to the recognition of objects, properties, or relations, in some patterns, are standard examples of coinstantiative representations. Animals constantly form such representations and so do we, a good deal of the time. As mental representations, coinstantiations are psychologically real and causally effective thoughts. Such thoughts have *their own* functional unity, as they represent more than a list of elements, in light of the cognitive role of the thoughts, their behavioral implications, and the goals they service. For a hungry cow, for instance, the visual coinstantiative judgment <green lawn ahead> has a motivational and behavioral unity that the separate recognition of lawn and greenness (say, in an experiment) would not have. But that unity is not of the predicative sort, because the P-dimensions are not involved.

From what was said so far, one may conclude that coinstantiation is the core of predication, so that predication would amount to coinstantiation plus. The syllogism behind this conclusion may run as follows. The S-dimensions are necessary for predication; coinstantiation also satisfies the S-dimensions; therefore, coinstantiation is necessary (though not sufficient) for, and thus is a constitutive part of, predication. Necessary in what sense, though? Logically or mentally? Logically, yes, any predication cannot fail to be a coinstantiation of thematic concepts. This is to say, more or less, that a predication cannot fail to have semantic content. If I think that the lawn is green, I cannot fail to conceptualize both the object <lawn> and its property <green>. In this logical sense, I can be said to think *of* a green lawn. But *psychologically*, no, emphatically no: the predicative judgment *that* the lawn is green is vastly different (P-different, that is) from a coinstantiative representation generated (say) by an animal mind. The mental coinstantiation and the predicative thought may converge on the same thematic categories, but mentally speaking, they link and employ them in quite different ways. A wasp and a wolf share a good number of properties, from genetic to phenotypic, but that does not make the wasp biologically necessary for and constitutive of the wolf.

In short, when a predication satisfies the same S-conditions as a coinstantiation, the overlap is necessarily logical but not mental. Even though a predication encodes information, classifies it under thematic categories, links the latter in some combinational fashion, and so on, down the S-list, it does so in a *mental* format vastly different from that of a coinstantiative thought, even though the latter, too, may satisfy the same S-conditions, yet in its *own* format and terms.

Transition

The thrust of the critical strategy in the next chapter will be twofold: to show that various theories of predication actually are theories of coinstantiation, logical or mental, but also that in such theories, coinstantiation is often confused with predication or taken to be sufficient for predication. This is because most accounts of predication adopt a structural and standard perspective, limiting themselves to the S-dimensions, which is why they are at best accounts of coinstantiation rather than of predication. As a result, even when they inquire psychologically into the competence for predication, these accounts at best explore the mental abilities involved in concept formation and application, the combinatorial syntax of mental representation, and so on, down the S-list. A few more pragmatically inclined theories gesture at some P-dimensions, but as we shall see, either do not go far enough toward explaining the mental competence for predication or go in the wrong direction.

2 Tales of Predication

This chapter is mostly about what predication is not, either not at all or partly not. Perhaps the chapter could have been better titled "Tales of Mispredication." Several influential philosophical and psychological views of predication are (briefly and, I admit, not too exegetically) examined in the search for clues and guidance to the mental competence itself. The search turns out not to be very successful. With the exception of the Fregean view, resolutely antipsychological, the other views surveyed form a fairly representative sample of psychologically sensitive theorizing about predication. Yet as far as I can tell, they either fail to recognize the P-dimensions of predication, or (usually as a result) mistake coinstantiation for predication (the Fregean, linguistic, and interpretative views as well as those about animal predication), or recognize some P-dimensions of predication but do not inquire into the underlying mental abilities (the pragmatic view), or else associate the key P-dimension of topic-comment-presupposition with the wrong mental abilities (such as attention).

2.1 Fregean Predication

Philosophers have done most of the thinking about predication, from the largely a priori perspectives of metaphysics, conceptual analysis, logic, language, and its ordinary use. The questions they asked about predication can be divided into five major areas: metaphysics (what about the structure of the world explains predication), language and other forms of representation (what conceptual, symbolic, and linguistic resources are needed to represent objects, events, properties, and relations in a predicative format), logic and grammar (formal and combinatorial requirements for predication), semantics (what predicative thoughts and sentences represent), and pragmatics (how predication may express the interests or perspectives of the predicators). The analyses made from these perspectives have produced important and insightful results, ably surveyed recently by Davidson (2005) and Gibson (2004). Yet as these authors conclude, for various reasons, all these analyses failed in their search for the elusive unity—and hence nature—of predication (although Davidson's and Gibson's diagnoses and solutions are different from mine).

Instead of canvasing these various a priori approaches, I will focus on some relevant aspects of Frege's conception of predication and treat it as a frame of reference for this chapter, for two reasons. First, this conception has been central to thinking about predication in recent analytic philosophy. Although framed in a novel way, the Fregean conception also echoes classical views about predication. Second, from its central position, the Fregean conception has influenced some psychological accounts of the competence for predication, as noted later in this chapter. My discussion of Frege on predication will be brief, sketchy, and unexegetical. I do not mean to dissect and evaluate it in its own territory of logic and semantics but rather to identify those theses that had an important impact on general and specifically psychological thinking about predication.

For the purposes of our discussion, three major axioms seem to have shaped Frege's view of predication (1891/1952). The first stipulates that a predicative thought is either directly expressed or indirectly identified by a sentence in a natural or formal language (or if we care to generalize, in some other symbol structure in some other code of representation). More exactly, a predicative thought is the propositional meaning or semantic content (or sense, as Frege calls it) of a complete sentence (or to generalize again, of some other symbol structure). This is a theme with many variations, which we do not need to attend to for our current discussion (Davidson 2005; Dummett 1973; Gibson 2004; Vieru 1997). We should note, in passing, that in Frege's view a thought (*Gedanke*) is not a mental particular (as is construed here) but a nonpsychological content or proposition. A judgment is a mental particular that acknowledges the truth of a thought, and an assertion is the expression of a judgment (Vieru 1997, 58). What is important for our purposes is that this axiom posits a compositional isomorphism between a sentence and the thought it expresses.

The second axiom concerns the format of predication. Consider, for example, the object-property format. According to Frege, the complete sense or meaning of a predicative sentence, and hence the thought it expresses, is made up of two parts: a concept, expressed by the predicate as a general term, and an object, referred to by the subject as a singular term. The concept-expressing predicate is incomplete or unsaturated, and the object-referring subject can complete or saturate it, thereby producing a complete sentence and hence a predicative thought. Frege thinks of predicate-expressed concepts as logical functions that map objects as arguments (i.e., whatever falls under singular terms) onto truth-values.

Frege's third axiom—the heart of his antipsychologism—is the notion that predication is best understood in terms of an ideal, abstract language, freed from the impurities and inexactitudes of a natural language, its grammar, and its communicative usage. It is an axiom that largely motivates the previous two. Frege thought that only an ideal language could fully satisfy the isomorphism axiom, so that the logical structure of the sentence can perfectly match that of the thought it expresses. He also thought that the saturated-unsaturated distinction underlying predication is a feature of the logical structure of the sentences of an ideal language, and differs from the variably implemented grammatical distinction between subject and predicate. Finally, Frege thought that linguistic communication and in particular the information conveyed grammatically by subjects and predicates, or pragmatically by topics and comments, have nothing to do with predication, as he construed it. In short, for Frege, predication has everything to do with the logical structure of an ideal language and nothing to do with psychology.

Major philosophical paradigms of recent decades, from phenomenology to the analytic philosophy of language and mind, have more or less bought into this Fregean stance on predication. But what they actually bought, I think, is logical coinstantiation, not predication. This is the kind of coinstantiation that satisfies the S-dimensions, and is indifferent to the underlying mental abilities and especially how thematic categories are blended in a thought. Frege seems to take the compositional isomorphism between a sentence and the thought it expresses to imply that the conceptual and formal resources of a sentence *suffice* to characterize the thought it expresses, and in particular its predicative format. This implication would bring only the S-dimensions into the analysis—in logical, not psychological terms.

I noted earlier that despite the novelty of the surrounding framework, Frege's conception preserves many classical insights about predication. Frege thinks of a concept as representing an incomplete or unsaturated universal that finds its completion or saturation when applied to a particular. This age-old notion practically builds predication into the very nature of concepts: to predicate is to saturate a concept; hence to be a concept is to be a potential predicate; conversely, to be a predicate is to be a concept attributed to or asserted about a particular object. According to the tradition and Frege as well, only properties or relations, thus universals, and not particulars, can be attributed or asserted. Since predication is attribution or assertion, going from universals to particulars, and since concepts express universals, concept application amounts to predication. This is no solution to the problem of predication, as many philosophers have observed [see note on Frege on predication]. Moreover, it reduces predication to concept instantiation.

But on my reading, concept application is no more than coinstantiation. If, in Fregean terms, a thought results from the application of concepts to particulars, then such a thought is merely a logical coinstantiation. And if, again in Fregean terms, a thought expresses a truth-valuable proposition, then the proposition is a minimal one, and hence the content of a logical coinstantiation. Psychologically speaking, if any application of a concept to its instances (its saturation) were predicative, we would find predication in most animal minds and computers too. The nature and unity of predication would marvelously cease to be a mystery.

I note in passing (but elaborate in chapter 5, section 5.4) that the Fregean notion of thought (and judgment as well) is quite unrealistic psychologically. This may not bother Frege and his philosophical disciples, but it should bother his psychological disciples. Both in cognition and communication, thoughts are more complex in the information they assume and convey than what is explicitly encoded in a sentence (or some other symbol structure). I do not mean only the P-dimensions of predication, deliberately missed by the Fregean paradigm, but also teleological dimensions, such as the goal and other utilities of a specific cycle of thinking, and other pragmatic dimensions, such as the Gricean strictures on brevity, informativeness, and so forth, which work both in cognition and communication.

Frege's bias against psychology and communication, and the adoption of an ideal formal language as a conceptual framework in which to think of predication, are best illustrated by the predicate calculus—rather misnamed, in my view, but not, presumably, in Frege's. The predicate calculus is psychologically neutral: it does not specify, nor does it care about, how the predicate is mentally related to its argument or object. The standard formula in the predicate calculus "Cx" (where "C" represents a property and "x" a variable object) or "Ca" (where "a" refers to a specific object) neither represents nor implies the predicative copula, or any other explicit indication of a predicate being mentally directed at or attributed to a subject; and it does not need to, for as noted in chapter 1, the mere joining or co-occurrence of "x" or "a" and "C," or the application of the latter to the former, would suffice for logical representation and inference. One does not need the P-dimensions to do predicate calculus or computer programming. As a speculative aside, I guess that artificial intelligence programs scripted along lines similar to the predicate calculus, as most of them are, would have little chance, if any, to emulate normal human thinking and communication. In any event, what Frege and his followers may have had in mind was "predication" à la "predicate calculus," which is a minimally propositional and logically coinstantiative "predication," and thus, in my eyes, no predication at all.

Frege seems to acknowledge the point, at least in part. He writes that "a distinction between subject and predicate finds no place in my representation of a judgment" chiefly because it does not affect the conceptual content of a judgment (Frege 1891/1952, paragraph 3; also cited in Gibson 2004, 144). This is a content that I take to be logically coinstantiative. Conceptually, the thought expressed by the sentence "this circle is round" is the same as the thought expressed by the sentence "this circle and round" or "this round circle." They all mean a logical coinstantiation of a property and an instance of it, as long as the distinction between property and instance is explicitly represented. The copula "is" is one of logical coinstantiation, *not* of predication. Even if a case can be made that a sentence needs the copula "is" (or some other cognate grammatical device) in order to apply a concept of a property to a particular object, or an action to an agent, the "is" in question need not be predicative. The point is that instead of being an infallible sign of predication, as it is so often taken to be, the use of the copula requires a prior and independent determination that the surrounding judgment is actually predicative. That determination cannot rely solely on the S-dimensions.

Transition

If, going beyond Frege but with the same assumptions, the predicate calculus were given a psychological reading, in terms of contents, it would not need much more than minimally propositional and coinstantiative representations of objects, properties, relations, and so on. This is precisely what we find, next, in several psychological accounts of predication. This is to say that many of these accounts buy into the assumption that the S-dimensions are not only necessary but also sufficient to explain predication psychologically. An implication of this assumption is that the facts that explain how minimal propositional contents represent what they do, according to the S-dimensions, are the same facts that explain why and how those contents are predicative. It is an implication that is not conducive to understanding predication as a mental competence and mental practice.

2.2 Linguistic Predication

Perhaps the best expression of a psychological version of the Fregean view, also widely adopted in cognitive science, is the notion that the basic resources of a natural or mental language, responsible for the S-dimensions, suffice to generate as well as explain predicative structures in thought and communication. I call this the *linguistic conception* and discuss it next.

Thoughts in Language

A symbolic code or language has at least two basic sets of resources: a vocabulary of symbols or words that activate the concepts employed in predications; and operations, under rules, that link such concepts in simple symbol structures or sentences, and form more complex such structures and sentences out of simple ones. Let us call a symbolic code or language with such resources *Ls*. Such an Ls could be either an underground mental language of thought (or mentalese) or a natural language, such as French. The difference is that unlike natural languages that operate only in human minds, the language of thought is supposed to work in many sorts of minds, animal and human, at all developmental stages, and is also supposed to underpin the acquisition of a natural language (Fodor 1975). It follows that if a language of thought is intrinsically predicative, then many animal species and human infants could in principle predicate. And if natural language is intrinsically predicative, then its speakers are predicators. I do not think that the antecedents of the last two conditional sentences are true, as the next paragraphs argue. I also think that there are other reasons, independent of mental or natural languages, why the consequents are also untrue, as the next sections of this chapter will show.

I assume that thoughts encoded in an Ls, whether animal or human, are structured in some formal patterns, are semantically determinate, and categorize thematically and separately objects, properties, relations, actions, and so on. In other words, I assume that the most pertinent conditions on the list S are met. My critique aims to show that an Ls-based mentation that satisfies the S-dimensions need not satisfy the P-dimensions and hence fails to be predicative.

The Elusive Descriptiveness

One argument is that there is nothing in the design of an Ls that would indicate that its thoughts are intended to describe states of affairs (the intended descriptiveness dimension), instead of representing how to do things (instrumentally), or in communication, giving orders or prompting some behavior (imperatively) or calling attention to something (signaling). A predicative thought assumes a deliberate descriptive stance in thinking and a declarative one in communication. Yet there is nothing in the design of an Ls, in its rules and regulations, that would distinguish among these various uses of thoughts, or that would favor the descriptive uses over the imperative or signaling ones. One can do with the grammar and logic of a language what one likes, descriptively, imperatively, instrumentally, or whatever. A natural language could be imperatively used, as it is most often in the military. As far as I can see, nothing in the list S rules out this possibility. Even when thoughts or utterances are used interrogatively or exclamatorily, they make predicative sense only if they presuppose the possibility of an intended descriptive usage. One cannot sensibly ask, "Is this essay written clearly?" or exclaim, "Mon Dieu, how clearly this essay is written!" unless one is prepared to entertain the predicative proposition that this essay is written clearly.

More important, even when the use of language is to represent some fact, the representation need not be predicative. A thought or utterance can represent, and be true of, items in the world or the relations among such items, without predicating anything. A coinstantiation will do just as well. Thematic coinstantiations emerge out of how organisms in general, not just people, spontaneously categorize and organize the input information, particularly from perception and memory. The result could be minimally descriptive and truth conditional without being predicative. Predication has no cognitive monopoly on representing facts and situations. Coinstantiation can do it as well, and much more frequently and spontaneously, and probably much more reliably, both in animal and human minds.

The Format Problem

Another critical question for the linguistic conception of predication is the following. How would a thinker, who relies *solely* on the S-resources of an Ls, know how to organize his predicative thoughts in a topic-comment-presupposition format, abstract the result from other things that his mind may attend to at the same time, and open such thoughts to further predicatively sensitive inferences? How would an Ls alone enable a thinker to *format* his predicative thoughts in such a manner, particularly if most predicative thoughts turn out to be organized differently from their surface grammatical and logical expressions? There is nothing I see in the conceptual and formal apparatus of an Ls that would tell a thinker how to construct a thought that satisfies the topic-comment-presupposition format. The rules and regulations of an Ls are combinatorial and generative, in that they can be applied repeatedly and in an immense variety of structures, which can implement predicative thoughts, but those rules and regulations contain no instructions for how to format such thoughts predicatively. They are instructions for expressing, not forming, predications.

The topic-comment-presupposition format is about what information to encode and organize explicitly, what to leave implicit or backgrounded and assumed, what to take as given, shared, or of interest, and what to add or contribute as a further classification or evaluation, how to enclose the result in a self-contained unit of thinking or communication, and how to make the result available to further mental operations. It may be argued that this formatting job may be done by simpler means than I am assuming here. For example, signaling or imperative communication may be organized in a background-foreground format by sensorimotor routines activated by a specific goal in a specific context. In a similar vein, one may claim that descriptive and perception-based thematic coinstantiations can handle the topic-comment-presupposition format by organizing and enclosing the thematic information in terms of one's attention or interest. I criticize these kinds of arguments in sections 2.3 and 2.5 below.

To sum up so far, an Ls may be the best medium of representation and computation in which to token and operate with predicative thoughts, by meeting the conditions on the list S. Yet the resources of an Ls fail to meet the conditions on intended directedness, topic-comment-presupposition format, and intended descriptiveness from the list P, and as a result fail to explain the nature and unity of predication.

2.3 Animal Predication

According to an influential version of linguistic conception—that of the language-of-thought hypothesis proposed by Jerry Fodor (1975)—animals and infants endowed with such a language could in principle predicate. If right, the critical arguments of the previous section invalidate such a conclusion. But there are other, more plausible psychological ways to make the case for animal and infant predication. In this and later sections I focus on several more attractive options.

Images Categorized

Consider first the structural composition of a thought, which is a basic S-dimension. Superficially, it may look as though animal (and perhaps infant) thoughts fail to have a compositional—and thus predicative—structure because their encoding is likely to be imagistic, hence analog, hence not parsed digitally into discrete parts. Suppose I see a big pink house. My visual image of the big pink house is not structured into distinct predicative components, for it does not single out the house as such, and separately, its bigness, and still separately, its pinkness. The bigness and pinkness of the house are imagistically coextensive with the house I see. Nor is my visual image as such propositional, for it does not relate the elements—house, pinkness, and bigness—in an explicitly represented pattern. No structuring into distinct components and no predication are ever effected by an image qua image. My visual image indiscriminately takes in the house, its size, color, and countless other details as well.

It would seem, then, that imagistic thoughts cannot have a structural composition. But this is not quite right. Thoughts are never just images. After all, children probably continue to think mostly imagistically for several years, and even adults think in imagistic thoughts a good deal of the time, and yet both groups also think structured thoughts, and actually impose a propositional format on many of their imagistic representations, as, for example, in mental imagery. Human children and adults, like all animals, use imagistic thoughts to provide useful discriminations that enable them to engage in various activities and pursue their goals. Mental resources other than images must operate on and with images to enable such activities and pursuits.

This is where *categorization* comes into the picture. All organisms apply a variety of categories to their perceptual inputs, images included, ranging from excitation thresholds, discriminations, and recognition patterns, to thematic categories and concepts. A visual image, such as that of big pink house in the midst of a scene, is normally brought under some recognitional pattern, and most likely structured into components under various thematic categories or concepts. Is this enough for animal or infant thoughts, assuming they are so structured, to qualify as predicative thoughts? Not quite, I think.

For one thing, the components categorized in animal or infant thoughts may be just coinstantiations. Suppose that a bird, able to recognize redness as a sign of danger, and also able to recognize the geometric and olfactive features of flowers as food, stumbles on a red flower and, although hungry, flees. Would we say that the bird recognizes <that the flower is red> and hence represents that fact predicatively? I think not. It is much more likely that the bird represents a coinstantiation of properties, with redness the most salient one and therefore causally preeminent, whence the fleeing. This reading is further motivated by the following consideration.

Most animals think not only imagistically but also motor-oriented thoughts—that is, thoughts that are intrinsically geared to action, and a specific context of opportunities or affordances for action. These are egocentric and instrumental how-to sorts of thoughts, rather than thoughts that represent nonegocentrically and noninstrumentally distal objects and properties—what we may call objectively descriptive thoughts. If such how-to thoughts have any structure, it is likely to be a structure designed to represent those aspects that can best guide action to a goal rather than to represent descriptively and objectively distal features of the world. Thus, although structured and categorized, sensorimotor thoughts would still fail to satisfy the requirements of intended objective descriptiveness and intended directedness, which are at the heart of predication.

Maybe what is missing from the picture so far are full-fledged concepts that zoom objectively on distal objects, properties, and relations, irrespective of context, appearance, and action, and also connect with other concepts in complex networks. Animals, from rats and pigeons to apes, seem able to recognize single objects and properties distally, in a variety of contexts and across several sensory modalities, which would suggest possession of concepts. These animals seem also able to link such concepts in some related patterns of thought that look almost like causal or analogical inferences (Dickinson and Shanks 1995; Tomasello and Call 1977). Nevertheless, like other forms of categorization, concepts can be applied in various ways, for various purposes. There is nothing intrinsically descriptive or predicative in their application. Setting aside well-known difficulties of defining what exactly animal (or human) concepts represent, and how they are applied, there is no argument (I know of) that is independent of the behavioral evidence of what animals recognize and act on, and that proves that the application of animal concepts is objective and intendingly descriptive, let alone predicative, as opposed to egocentric, action bound, and instrumental.

Yet there are other ways to make a case for the predicative character of animal thoughts. I focus on two accounts that I regard as among the most insightful and systematic. One, discussed next, appeals to a specific thematic design of animal categories, and the other, examined in section 2.5, appeals to perception.

The Right Categories

What I call the *right-categories account* endeavors to show the presence in an animal or infant mind of the right thematic categories of object, property, and relation (and possibly others), and then to demonstrate the resulting presence of subject-predicate judgments under such categories. One of the most sustained and comprehensive attempts to demonstrate the predicativeness of animal thoughts in terms of the right categories is that of Jose Bermudez (2003).

As I understand it, the basic idea is to show that many animal species (at least, from rats on) operate mentally with what looks like or is best explained as a subject-predicate structure. How does one determine the presence of such a predicative structure? Essentially, by establishing that the animal represents objects separately from representing properties. That, in turn, requires establishing that the animal has thematic categories of objects as persisting physical bodies, distinct from their variable properties. Such object-categories, perceptual in nature, enable the animal to detect regularities governing physical objects, such as solidity, persistence, invariance of size and volume, movement, causal powers, and so on. An animal that has such object-categories may be said to possess (what psychologists call) a naive physics, at least a naive physics of objects as bodies with various properties. This conclusion suggests that the animal's thoughts are structured predicatively because, as Bermudez (2003, 59) writes, "The thoughts attributed [to the animal] have an internal structure that perceptions do not have. The ability to represent a given object as having a given property goes together with the ability to represent that object as potentially having a range of properties, and, moreover, with the ability to represent that property as holding of a range of further objects."

Let us grant the idea—not implausible from an evolutionary angle—that many animal species (certainly inquisitive mammals) have a naive physics that represents bodies invariantly and independently of the context and action, and distinctly from representing the properties and relations that these bodies may have. Let us also grant the bolder idea that the naive-physical categories of bodies have the potential of identifying possible subjects in a predicative thought. Does it follow that this potential becomes reality in some animal minds? Not quite. As Bermudez (2003, 69) himself notes in a different context, "It is clear that the simultaneous tokening in the mind of a property representation and an object representation is not sufficient to generate the thought that the object in question has the property in question—hence to determine the relevant truth condition. . . .

This is of course the traditional problem of the unity of the proposition . . . or the binding problem for thoughts." Well said.

More than a simultaneous tokening of the categories of objects and properties—thus more than coinstantiation—is therefore needed. Since Bermudez thinks that an animal's naive physics identifies objects as potential subjects, the remaining task is to ascertain how the animal represents properties that could occupy the predicate position. His explanation focuses on those thought components that show up in different thoughts about fixed objects, thereby indicating that the animal's representations of properties and relations are projectable, and as such can explain its behaviors in a variety of circumstances. This analysis suggests that the representations of properties and relations (as potential predicates) are representational constancies, under appropriate property- and relation-categories, on a par with those made possible by the animal's object-categories (the potential subjects).

I will not go into the details of Bermudez's insightful analysis because my critique does not depend on them, as far as I can see, and also because I agree that the analysis could map out plausibly the properties and relations that the animal represents. The critical question is whether the analysis *also* explains the intended directedness and objective descriptiveness that are at the core of predication. I doubt it, for several reasons.

To begin with, an animal's categories of objects and projectable properties may still be jointly or successively applied in patterns that fail to approximate the P-dimensions. The result, again, could be just thematic coinstantiations. I see nothing in Bermudez's account to rule out this possibility. It is not the categories of objects and properties, no matter how projectable and versatile, that define predication but, primarily, the intended directedness relation going from the content of the predicate category to an instance of the subject category in a topic-comment-presupposition format. As far as I can see, Bermudez's analysis does not establish the presence of this pattern in animal minds.

As for the intently and nonegocentrically descriptive format of predication, my objection is that animal thinking is likely to be imperative, and geared entirely to how to behave and achieve results, as is the case with infant mentation. In that case, its naive-physical categories can be said to represent the animal's world in ways that tell it how to behave toward physical objects—for example, not to bump into some but to eat others. Animal categories in general are more plausibly construed as behavioral categories that discriminate and classify information to the extent to which, and in the format in which, they guide the animal's actions and reactions in its physical and social environments (Bogdan 1994, 1997). The same can be said about the representations of object-property coinstantiations: they tell the animal how to behave toward specific environmental arrangements.

In short, the job of the animal's naive physics, with its representations of projectable properties, is likely to be instrumental and action bound, sponsoring how-to thoughts rather than nonegocentrically descriptive thoughts-that. The fact that an animal's naive-physical categories of objects and projectable properties go beyond what perception reveals, toward some ontological invariants, even in the complex form of thematic coinstantiations, does not mean that the job of those categories is other than guiding action. It simply means that the semantics of the animal cognition may be distal, and that therefore the animal has a better mental grasp of and guidance toward its goals than animals whose cognitive semantics is stimuli bound and hence proximal (Bogdan 1994).

Bermudez's analysis provides a thoughtful and detailed defense of the idea of the structural composition of animal thoughts as well as the distal reach of their categories, at least in many mammalian species. According to the distinction made in chapter 1, such animal coinstantiative thoughts may also be minimally propositional. Yet as far as I can tell, Bermudez's analysis fails to establish the predicativeness of animal thoughts [see note on Reification of Animal Propositions].

As the title of his book *Thoughts without Words* indicates, Bermudez aimed to show that there are predicative thoughts without words. In my view, the only wordless thoughts are coinstantiative. As argued later, thoughts are predicative not because they can be expressed only by words but because, antecedently, it is the very acquisition of words, in some specific manner, that enable thoughts to become predicative.

I take the views surveyed in this section, and the one based on the language of thought from a previous section, to be among the most serious, powerful, and systematic, yet I think they fail to make the case for animal or infant predication. There are other views that favor animal predication (e.g., Carruthers 2005; Dickinson and Shanks 1995; Seyfarth 2005). I take their arguments, often similar to those discussed earlier, to establish at most the presence in animal and infant minds of thematic categories and their various coinstantiations, including their minimally propositional versions. So the same critical verdict would apply.

2.4 Interpretative Predication

This section concludes the survey of the views that take the S-dimensions to be necessary and sufficient for predication, thereby (on my analysis) reducing predication to coinstantiation. Unlike the previous sections, this one does not have a visible, fixed, and clearly authored target. Rather, canvasing several sources, it reconstructs a possible line of thinking about propositional thoughts and, by implication, predication.

As a preview, the rough idea is the following. The notion of proposition is an invention of folk psychology and does not pick out an intrinsic pattern in the mind. It is, to paraphrase Davidson (2001), an "object before the mind" and not an "object in the mind." So when we think and theorize about propositional thoughts, we do it with a folk-psychological model in mind—the model of the object before the mind. On this model, the folk psychologist construes propositional thoughts solely in terms of their semantic content alone—that is, in terms of what they represent or are true of, hence along the S-dimensions only, and therefore (on my analysis) as logical coinstantiations. Intriguingly, some theorists go a step further and suggest that propositional thoughts, as folk-psychological concoctions, somehow manage to get internalized as intrinsic patterns in the mind, thus morphing from objects before the mind into objects in the mind. As a result, again on my analysis, propositional "predications" but actually mental coinstantiations get to run the psyche. This is the basic idea; now some details.

The Invented Proposition

I begin with a distinction: one *has* thoughts, but one (perhaps only a human) can also *represent* thoughts, those of others and one's own. In the first position, one is a thinker whose thoughts represent something or other. In the second position, one reports or describes thoughts, as in quotation or reported speech, or figures out or interprets someone else's thoughts. One is a reporter or interpreter of thoughts, respectively, in this second position—in short, one is a folk psychologist who metarepresents thoughts, because one represents (thinks about) other representations (thoughts). I will use the notions of interpretation and folk psychology, and their grammatical variations, interchangeably.

There is an influential philosophical doctrine, called eliminativism (for reasons we do not have to go into here), positing that propositions, as contents of thoughts, are literally creations of folk psychology. This version of eliminativism, well articulated by Paul Churchland (1979), contends that propositions are metarepresentational constructs employed for conceptualizing the propositional contents of attitudes, such as desires and beliefs, and using such concepts in folk-psychological explanations and predictions. The concepts are useful and successful in this interpretative job, but have no mental counterpart. They are not part of the ontology of minds.

The favorite analogy of the eliminativist is the notion of number. Numbers are conceptual concoctions used to quantify and explain physical phenomena. Their explanatory usefulness and success need not entail that numbers actually exist in the physical world. The same, we are told, is true of propositions as alleged contents of thoughts: they are conceptual posits that exist *before* the interpretative mind, which is the mind of a folk psychologist, but not *in* the mind as such—the mind of a thinker. In short, propositions, like numbers, are clever inventions that enable folk psychologists and scientists (respectively) to map out as well as talk about entities and regularities of the mental and physical domains (respectively). But their ontological reification is unwarranted.

This eliminativist analysis can be extended to the interpretation of our own thoughts, courtesy of Wilfrid Sellars's ingenious thought experiment (1956/1963) intended to explain how we come to understand our own thoughts. Sellars suggests that the notion of propositional thought begins as a public construct of folk psychology. This is because how and what we think about the thoughts of others is determined by the semantics of the public language in which we describe those thoughts, and the role such descriptions play in reporting, interpreting, and explaining what other people think, say, and do. At some point in evolution, according to Sellars, this folk-psychological strategy turns to one's own thoughts and attitudes, not just for explanation, but for literal description as well. People thus come to think of their own thoughts in terms of the public semantics of the language of folk psychology.

Evolutionary details aside, Sellars makes an important point: when we report, describe, or quote our thoughts—as opposed to just having them—we usually metarepresent them in the same terms in which we metarepresent the thoughts of others. There is a rather wide consensus in the psychological literature on this matter (Astington, Harris, and Olson 1988; Bartsch and Wellman 1995; Perner 1991). Without elaboration here, it seems the right consensus because, I think, metarepresenting our own thoughts is part of mental self-regulation, which can be adaptive and effective only in public terms that represent shareable facts and situations (Bogdan 1997, 2010).

Eliminativism seems to me right about one fundamental fact: namely, that the public and linguistic terms in which people, as folk psychologists, normally conceptualize and talk about thoughts and attitudes, about their propositional contents, need not be—and most often are not—the terms in which people think in general (Stich 1983; also Bogdan 1993, 1997). The salutary message of eliminativism, therefore, is not to take the metarepresentations of folk psychology as necessarily matching or revealing the design and operation of the human mind. This message applies to predication as well: people think predicatively, most of the time, but reporting or interpreting—that is, metarepresenting folk psychologically—their thoughts need not always reveal the predicative design of their thinking.

Metarepresenting Coinstantiations

Assuming, then, with eliminativism and Sellars, that the propositional contents of thoughts are public creatures of folk psychology, the question is what is the format of these contents. A plausible case can be made that in reporting, describing, or interpreting thoughts, and thus in adopting the stance of a folk psychologist, one is primarily interested in what the thoughts in question represent, inform about, and therefore are true of—namely, facts, events, and situations. This can be done by metarepresenting the semantic contents of the reported or interpreted thoughts in terms of the truth conditions of the expressions of those thoughts, and if necessary, the ways in which those facts, events, and situations are conceptualized (Barwise and Perry 1983; Davidson 1984; also Bogdan 1989, 1993, 1997). This is to say that the semantic contents of reported or interpreted thoughts are normally metarepresented in terms of S-dimensions, and hence as logical coinstantiations. The thinker may be a predicator, and most of the time is, but his thoughts are metarepresented by the folk psychologist *only* as logical coinstantiations—logical, because the folk psychologist is usually uninterested in the specifics of the thinker's mental representations.

To take an example, suppose I ask you about the weather tomorrow, and you answer—and I interpret your answer as reflecting your belief—that it will rain tomorrow. As a folk psychologist, I metarepresent the semantic content of the linguistic expression of your belief, which is the thought that it will rain tomorrow, as a future state of affairs—say, <rain tomorrow>. This is what I am interested in—namely, information that joins one event, rain, and a time period, tomorrow. A logical coinstantiation construed in S-terms suffices. Your answer may have had the explicit predicative form of "tomorrow will be rainy," but could also have been "Tomorrow? Rainy!" or just "Rain," with the same informative effect. Unless the context requires it, the folk psychologist need not attend to the psychopragmatic matrix in which occur the thoughts being reported or interpreted. In the example, I may have animated my metarepresentation of your belief that it will rain tomorrow in predicative terms (perhaps when remembering and rephrasing it later), but as a folk psychologist, I was initially indifferent to whether you actually predicated it or not. I was solely interested in what your belief represented—the possible state of affairs itself—and not in the particulars of how you represented it.

Likewise, when we attribute thoughts to animals, we take a similarly reportive or interpretative stance, resulting in attributing logical coinstantiations as semantic contents of those animal thoughts, perhaps modulated by some empirical constraints. Thus, for instance, when I interpret the dog as thinking that the cat is up in the tree, I project what I know about dogs (that they have their categories of cat, tree, climbing, hiding, etc.) and this dog's current behavior as a coinstantiative representation of a state of affairs <cat up in the tree>. My projection employs only some S-dimensions, adjusted to what I know (or is generally known) about dog mentation and behavior. As it happens, animals (unlike people) actually *are* only mental coinstantiators of various sorts, even though how they actually coinstantiate as well as the nature of the functional unity of their mental coinstantiations are beyond the grasp and interest of folk psychology.

The point that matters here is that if the analyst of predication construes thoughts on the model of reported or interpreted thoughts, and therefore adopts the metarepresentational stance of folk psychology, then the analysis is likely to focus solely on the semantic contents of thoughts along the S-dimensions. Folk psychology thus tends to portray predication as logical coinstantiation. Many analyses of predication, including some discussed in this chapter, seem to have regarded predication from such a folk-psychological stance. In general, we tend to think of thoughts and attitudes in folk-psychological terms, and have intuitions about them in the same terms. The very notions of thought and attitudes, such as desire and belief, are creatures of folk psychology. Many years ago, I noted that one does not find these notions in texts or articles of cognitive psychology, as technical notions that are defined theoretically and employed in analyses or experiments (Bogdan 1983). The last time I checked, the situation has not changed. In contrast, one would find the notions of desire or belief on almost every page of psychology texts about folk psychology, which is precisely the point.

To conclude, then, as folk psychologists, both ordinary and philosophical folk, including the readers of this page, are intuitively inclined to think of thoughts and propositional attitudes in folk-psychological terms. For good reasons, these terms tend to represent reported, described, or interpreted thoughts, human or animal, as logical coinstantiations. For much less good reasons, adopted by many philosophical or psychological analyses of thoughts, the folk-psychological stance tends to take logical coinstantiation to define the essence of predication.

The Metamorphosis

I noted that eliminativism is right about the fundamental fact that the terms in which folk psychology conceptualizes thoughts are not necessarily the terms in which people actually think. But I think eliminativism is wrong about two other fundamental facts. One is that folk psychology is far from being just a prototheoretical piece of folklore (on a par, as is often said, with folk astronomy or folk medicine) invented to rationalize and predict the mundane interactions among people. At its core, folk psychology is a basic mental competence, with a likely history of natural selection (Bogdan 1997). The other fundamental fact that eliminativism is wrong about is that folk psychology, or rather portions of it, play a major role in designing human thinking. Far from being just the work of neural networking, some basic mental syntax, or some general-purpose inference engine, as many eliminativists and other theorists assume, human thinking is designed during development by a variety of abilities, including those of folk psychology, to operate in specific formats. As an outcome of this multiconvergent development, predication is one such format, as we shall see. Assuming that this is true—a promissory note to be redeemed in the next few chapters—the question then is how to construe this design role of folk psychology with respect to predication.

One influential idea of how folk psychology may redesign human thinking is that of a *metamorphosis*, from how we think about minds to how we think in our own minds. This idea was anticipated philosophically. Davidson (1984, 157), for example, has famously opined that "a creature cannot have thoughts unless it is an interpreter of the speech of another." The suggestion is that one cannot be a thinker, or a believer in particular, unless one is a folk psychologist. This is because, as argued by Grice (1957) and acknowledged by Davidson (1984, 158), one cannot be a speech interpreter unless one is an interpreter of mental states, and hence a folk psychologist. Davidson is also known for the somewhat related (and rather extravagant) claim that one cannot have beliefs unless one has the concept of belief, and thus unless (again) one is a folk psychologist.

Whereas Sellars's position, as I read it, is that one cannot *metarepresent* (think and talk about) thoughts unless one speaks a language in whose semantic terms one interprets other minds, Davidson's point, which is much stronger, seems to be that one cannot *have* propositional thoughts unless the same conditions of folk-psychological interpretation hold. It is a further implication of Davidson's view that not being linguistic interpreters of other minds, animals and human infants do not have propositional thoughts. Since people have thoughts, attitudes, and also folk-psychological concepts, it appears that the propositions before the interpretative mind of a folk psychologist somehow manage to morph into the mentalized propositional contents of his thoughts. How would that work?

One brave developmental psychologist has ventured the notion that such a morphing does actually take place in childhood. Echoing the ideas of Sellars and Davidson, David Olson suggests a developmental metamorphosis of folk psychology into a modus operandi of the cognitive mind itself. Olson (1988, 420) writes that "children actually acquire the cognitive machinery that makes intentional state ascription literally true of them at a certain stage in development. . . . A cultural form, a folk psychology, acquired by the child as a theory of mind, may be instrumental in making those mental states [beliefs and desires] subject to awareness and deliberate control." He also notes that the folk psychology of belief and other attitudes (as envisaged instrumentalistically by Quine, Daniel Dennett, Sellars, and Davidson) acquires through development a mental reality of sorts: "we, in constructing beliefs, make up our minds" (Olson 1989, 620).

Olson's metamorphosis idea reflects a more general theme, well expressed by Peter Hobson (1993, 185), that "the development of the child's own mind is bound up with her increasingly sophisticated awareness of 'other minds.' . . . The very structure and functioning of the mind may alter as a result of new understandings about the mind itself." I called this the *minding-minds* theme—minds that redesign themselves and acquire new resources by virtue of minding (i.e., interpreting) other minds (Bogdan 2000, 2001). Predication, I will argue in the next chapters, is an important variation on this theme, but its redesign turns out not to be the outcome of a single or domain-specific metamorphosis originating in folk psychology. The story of predication is going to be more complex than that.

The question now is what format of propositional thought is delivered by Olson's metamorphosis proposal. (As noted in chapter 5, Olson has further interesting ideas about the development of predication, but they do not touch directly on the role of folk psychology, which is of concern at this point.) Read literally, Olson's idea of a developmental metamorphosis seems to follow the Sellars-Davidson position by adopting the stance of folk psychology. The problem here, and not a small one, is that young children become predicators around the age of two and hence much before they can interpret complex propositional attitudes, such as beliefs and intentions, a few years later. A finer distinction is needed, inviting a reformulation of Olson's proposal.

The distinction I think we need, in order to understand both the development of folk psychology and its role in designing predicative minds, is between naive psychology and folk psychology. *Naive psychology* is a largely innate ability, exercised since early childhood and geared mostly to visible relations between people, and between people and items in the world, such as gazing, seeing, and emoting. Folk psychology, exercised a few years later, and geared to more complex and less overt mental states, such as opinions, hopes, and intentions, builds on naive psychology yet adds new interpretative tools, such as cultural norms, patterns of language use, and the massive use of imagination, inference, and mental reconstruction (Bogdan 1997, 2003) [see note on Naive versus Folk Psychology]. So far, the discussion—revolving around eliminativism, Davidson, Sellars, and Olson's developmental proposal—was about the interpretative stance of *folk* psychology and its tendency to posit logical coinstantiations as semantic contents of interpreted or reported thoughts. But when we turn to early childhood, during which the earlier and simpler *naive* psychology reigns supreme, the picture changes significantly, with major implications for understanding the development of predication. For it is this early naive (not the later folk) psychology that is involved in the development of predicative thinking, as we shall see beginning with the next chapter.

2.5 Perceptual Predication

I have examined so far several accounts of predication that more or less reduce predication to S-dimensioned coinstantiation, logical or mental, or at least leave open the door to such a reduction. The next two kinds of accounts—perceptual and pragmatic—begin to identify aspects of the P-dimensions of predication. The perceptual story has it that the predicative structure of thoughts, including the thoughts of animals and human infants, somehow emerges out of how (mostly visual) perception works. I will consider two versions of this option—one that focuses on the work of the dorsal and ventral circuits of vision, but risks the threat of coinstantiation, and another, more promising, that concentrates on perceptual attention, with the aim of locating the source of the topic-comment format of propositional predication.

Dorsal-Ventral Predication

A recent and ingenious analysis aims to ground the roots of predication in distinct neural pathways—one that locates objects in a body-centered space, and the other that attributes properties to objects (Hurford 2005). In visual perception these are the dorsal and the ventral pathways, respectively (Milner and Goodale 1995). James Hurford's basic idea is that PREDICATE(x), which he calls a "predicate-argument structure," is a schematic representation of the brain's integration of two processes—the indexical location of an object (the dorsal job), and the semantic representation of its perceived properties (the ventral job). A predicate, in his view, "corresponds, to a first approximation, to a judgment that a creature can make about an object. . . . [T]he predicate represents some judgment about the argument, which is canonically an attended-to object" (Hurford 2005, 264, 270). Furthermore, "the syntactic structure of PREDICATE(x) formula combines the two types of term [i.e., predicate and its argument] into a unified whole capable of receiving a single interpretation which is a function of the denotations of the parts; this whole is typically taken to be an event or a state of affairs in the world" (267). So construed, predicative structures, to be found in nonhuman primates and possibly other mammals, preexist language and provide the neural platform for predication in language (263, 267).

My assessment of this interesting proposal is rather similar to that of Bermudez's, from section 2.3 above: it establishes at best the presence and operation of thematic coinstantiations (of the object-property sort), but not of predications. One major difference between the two analyses is that the naive physics, posited by Bermudez to detect objects, operates nonegocentrically and distally, whereas the indexical object-detection by dorsal means operates egocentrically and proximally, as probably does the ventral representation of properties, at least in many animal minds (Anderson and Oates 2005). Even more than Bermudez's animal predicators, Hurford's perceptually egocentric predicators most likely represent only action-bound thematic coinstantiations. A perceptually egocentric and action-bound animal brain is unlikely to bootstrap itself into a predicative brain, and has no obvious evolutionary reasons to do so, as I suggest in later chapters.

Predication by Attention

One's attention isolates something of interest in the foreground from what one is marginally aware of in the background. Attention also separates new from given information, or what one focuses on from what one takes for granted or presupposes. For our purposes here, I take the background-foreground and new-given information distinctions as more or less equivalent. A neat psychological solution to the problem of predication—or at least parts of it—may be in the offing, if these attention-driven distinctions can be somehow parlayed conceptually into subject-predicate structures.

Elizabeth Bates (1976) has produced one of the most cogent versions of this line of analysis in an insightful, well-argued, and systematic work on language acquisition, one of the best, on which I will draw in later chapters. She frames the argument in terms of the topic-comment structure, which she takes to be equivalent to the foreground-background or new-given information as well as a precursor of linguistic predication. Bates thinks that the development of topic-comment structure is entirely or mostly endogenous and centered on attention. The basic idea is that registered at the sensorimotor level, aspects of the environment provide the topic and the organism's attention the comment. This hypothesis leads, unsurprisingly, to the claim that "if animal signals are viewed as procedures that comment on situational topics, then human propositions are not a new breed, but rather the same topic-comment relations. . . . The human one-year-old can be viewed as halfway between animal and human adult signal systems" (Bates 1976, 105). (I will object to the antecedent, for I do not think that animal signals literally comment on anything.) It is not surprising, either, that Bates quotes with approval the suggestion that predicative structures are innate (106). After all, so is the capacity for attention in nonhuman as well as human animals.

A first and somewhat simplistic question that springs immediately to mind is the following: If the topic-comment format is one of solitary adaptation of attention to targets of sensorimotor behaviors, why haven't other animal species and particularly nonhuman primates, all endowed with attention, evolved not only predication but also some of its cognitive implications, such as declarative communication, and perhaps language and abstract thinking? And if, as Bates also maintains, the development of predicative abilities is one of learning and internal sensorimotor restructuring through Piagetian assimilation and accommodation, which are forms of learning that may be open to other species as well, certainly primates, then, again, why is it that only humans benefited from the potential represented by the topic-comment structure?

These questions may be unfair because Bates actually thinks that animal minds are able to predicate in a rudimentary way, but lacking a natural language, they miss the symbolic form of predication and its far-reaching cognitive implications. If what she means is that animal thoughts may have minimal propositional contents, as coinstantiations, along the lines suggested by my earlier reading of Bermudez's account, then I think this is possible. Yet Bates's view of symbolization and reference seem to go for predication proper, and thus raise the same objections as those against Bermudez.

As for the origin of animal predication, Bates (1976, 103) observes that "the very first acts of reference, even prior to speech, grow out of a pattern of fixed orientation to a novel stimulus . . . an attentional capacity certainly present in lower species and present very early in humans," and adds that "if, as our evidence indicates, the first speech acts build on the child's solitary attentional responses, then he will naturally encode what has drawn his attention" (104). Both observations, about the first acts of reference and speech, may be true, yet they do not add up to predication. As I will have occasion to note later, the child 's first words, at around six months, are learned by association, leading to linguistic coinstantiations rather than predications. But during the most productive period of word acquisition, beginning in the twelve- to eighteen-months' interval, the child relies much less on salience-driven attention than on figuring out the coreferential intent of the adult introducing the new word explicitly (Sabbagh and Baldwin 2005). The latter, according to the argument of later chapters, is going to be the platform for predication.

I think that Bates's analysis of predication in terms of the topic-comment-presupposition format is the right way to go. But I do not think it is a format generated by solitary perceptual attention. The latter does format representations in foreground-background and new-given information terms. These are *not*, however, the topic-comment terms, as I understand them. True, a comment often provides new or foreground information, reflects one's attention, and in communication, is meant to capture the attention of an addressee. Yet this is because, *antecedently*, the essential function and intent of a comment is to cause a mental effect in an audience by targeting a topic and having the audience recognize this intent.

(This line of analysis will be taken up in chapter 4.) This most critical dimension of predication—of a comment intently directed at a topic—remains unexplained in terms of solitary attention.

It is worth recalling at this point that autistic people have an unimpaired perceptual attention (just as they have the right categories of objects, properties, and relations), yet their mastery of topic-comment predication in communication is frequently impaired. This is significant because, as noted in later chapters, the topic-comment structure *first* emerges in communication and only later is emulated in one's own thinking (Hobson 1993; also Bogdan 2000). (Conceivably, autistic people who systematically fail to follow a conversation, by failing to track its topic-comment-presupposition patterns, may also fail to predicate, at least in the normal way, despite handling competently other aspects of their language, grammar included. In that eventuality, their use of the copula "is" and its cognates may simply reflect coinstantiations, no matter how complex. This is a hypothesis worth pursuing, but I know of no empirical evidence to support it.)

Once operative, a topic-comment structure does engage one's attention toward the comment, making it salient in the foreground and leaving the topic in the background. This is because the comment usually contributes new information or introduces an attitude to information, and attention gravitates toward new information or a new attitude, whereas the topic is given or already known. This is to say that the topic-comment structure can generate a given-new information structure, but not conversely. Not every given-new (or background-foreground) information structure has a topic-comment format. Any movement of the head, for example, will provide visual perception with the former, though not the latter. The key difference, on my analysis, is that a comment is mentally directed at a topic, whereas new (or foreground) information need not be directed at given (or background) information.

Finally, I think that Bates's account pays a price here for a programmatic Piagetian outlook that emphasizes the solitary mind and its sensorimotor abilities to act on the physical world. In contrast, I think that topic-comment-presupposition and later linguistic predication develop only out of social interaction and communication. In the present survey, Bates's is nevertheless the first sustained effort to address in psychological terms a key pragmatic parameter of predication. I conclude the survey with some philosophical views that also discern an intrinsically pragmatic format of predication, around the topic-comment structure, but do not explore its psychological roots.

2.6 Pragmatic Predication

Decades ago and more recently as well, several philosophers and linguists developed a pragmatic conception that analyzes the topic-comment infrastructure of perception, thinking, and discourse, and implicitly that of predication (Clark and Clark 1977; Dretske 1969, 1972; Gibson 2004; Sperber and Wilson 1986). A few philosophical accounts are explicit about the pragmatic topic-comment-presupposition format of predication.

John Cook Wilson (1926) and Frank Ramsey (1925) were early philosophical advocates of a pragmatic view of predication. Ramsey took the position that it is the interest with which one approaches the description of a fact or situation that determines what counts as subject and predicate, respectively. For Cook Wilson, the subject-predicate distinction is not intrinsically metaphysical, logical, or grammatical but rather reflects the contrast between old or given information (the subject) and new information (the predicate) in communication; and this contrast in turn reflects the interest and knowledge of the speaker and hearer.

Following the (rather undeveloped) insights of Cook Wilson and Ramsey, Martha Gibson (2004, particularly chapter 7) develops a rich and systematic explanation of the pragmatics of predication in terms of the topic-comment format. Although starting from a communicational perspective, Gibson's strategy is to ground the pragmatic asymmetry between subject and predicate, and their propositional unity in a sentence, in a dependence relation between what causes the occurrences of the predicate and the subject. Those causes in turn are regarded as constituents of states of affairs that occasion the utterances of the subject and predicate. Although aware that the occasioning of those utterances involves the mental states of the utterer and interlocutor, Gibson prefers a *nonpsychological* explanation that captures—whereas, she holds, the psychological explanation "obscures"—the ontological structures involved, such as objects, properties, and the like. Another reason for this preference may be to avoid the Gricean strategy of grounding semantic properties of sentences in the semantic properties of mental states. Since what needs to be explained is why and how an utterance manages to express a predicative proposition, Gibson's worry about the Gricean strategy is circularity: the strategy posits that a sentence means propositionally what a speaker means propositionally, and the speaker's meaning results from the intent, in uttering the sentence, to produce a belief in an audience; that belief, presumably, is *already* propositional, in a predicative and unitary way (Gibson 2004, 142, 153). I return to this (unwarranted) worry shortly.

I find Gibson's overall approach insightful and in many respects congenial to the one developed here. The pragmatic topic-comment-presupposition format is a crucial P-dimension that points to the mental design of the competence for predication. Gibson is primarily interested in the unity of the proposition rather than the psychology of predication, and to that end, she uses the topic-comment format to project causal dependencies among structural facts in the outside, extramental world. True, the structural facts do reveal causal dependencies among the referents of the topic and comment terms, and predication must respect these dependencies to be true and informative. The same, however, is true of coinstantiation: it, too, must represent objective relations, often causal, among the referents of the joint representations. So as noted frequently earlier, the difference between coinstantiation and predication cannot be just an objective, ontological one. Indeed, it seems to me that the very projection from the topic-comment format to causal dependencies among structural facts in the world is first made mentally by the predicator—and inferentially by an interlocutor or reader. And the question—the psychological question of this book—is what enables one to make such a mental projection and in general to predicate.

This observation leads to another one about Gibson's approach. She was said to worry about the circularity that a Gricean approach would smuggle into the analysis of the predicative proposition. This concern may affect a conceptual approach to the unity problem, which is Gibson's project, but not a psychological explanation of predication, which is my project. In fact, the whole point of this book is that we cannot understand how and why our minds predicate unless we examine the formation and work of the competence involved. More to the point, however, is that a developmental reinterpretation of Grice's analysis of meaning need not assume any prior grasp of beliefs, propositions, or language itself. As communicators, young children intend and manage to produce mental effects in others, and also recognize the communicative intents of others in the same terms, without appeal to explicitly propositional beliefs or other attitudes. There is, therefore, no threat of circularity. This is a promissory note to be redeemed in chapter 4, section 4.1.

Summation and Implications

The moral of the story, so far, is that representing the world in terms of thematic categories of objects, properties, relations, agents, actions, and so forth, is necessary but not sufficient for predication. Nor does predication emerge naturally from the exercise of a language, whether mental or natural.

Perceptual attention may structure information in ways that are exploited by predication but is not inherently predicative. The complementary work of dorsal and ventral perception may provide an early neural platform for perceptual coinstantiations of the object-property or agent-action kinds, but those coinstantiations are a long way from predications. Folk psychology may posit propositions in its ascriptions of thoughts and attitudes, and to the extent that it redesigns the mind, it may bring propositions in the operation of the mind. But the question still is whether the propositions are minimal and coinstantiative, or genuinely predicative. Also, as noted in chapters 4 and 5, it is the earlier version of naive psychology that begins to redesign the child's mind much before the child is able as a folk psychologist to ascribe full-fledged propositional attitudes, such as beliefs or intentions.

One could retort that my critical survey, far from being exhaustive, has not shown that animals or infants cannot possibly think and communicate predicatively but rather that a convincing theoretical and empirical case for animal or infant predication has not yet been made in the literature examined here. Fair enough. But in the light of the arguments of the next chapters, I think it will also be fair to anticipate that a plausible case against animal and infant predication *can* be made. With this anticipation in mind, it is reasonable to consider several implications of what was argued so far, which sets the stage for what follows.

First, if it is not animal, predication is likely to be exclusively human. But second, if not present in the infant mind, predication must emerge later in childhood. Third, given that all the accounts criticized in this chapter more or less advocate the innateness of predicative structures in the animal and human minds, but given the emergence of these structures in later childhood, *after* the factors invoked by the accounts in question have been operative for some time, it is reasonable to infer that the ability to predicate might not be innate, in the strong sense of being blueprinted in the genome. Yet fourth, the ability to predicate is a human universal, which suggests that it may not be simply learned but rather piggyback on other universal and possibly innate traits as well as abilities. And fifth, since predication was shown not to be inherent in the thematic categories of objects, properties, and relations, and their coinstantiations, nor in the formal resources of a mental or natural language, nor in the operation of perception and attention (all more or less pointing to S-dimensions), those universal traits and abilities that initially feed into the ability to predicate are likely to reside in noncategorical, nonperceptual, nonlinguistic, and nonformal areas of human mental development. These are the central implications developed and defended in the remainder of this book.

II Toward an Explanation

3 A Hypothesis

The point of philosophy is to start with something so simple as not to seem worth stating, and to end with something so paradoxical that no one will believe it.

—Bertrand Russell

Although I am not practicing philosophy as Russell understood it, certainly not here, I take his remark to be an apt description of the central hypothesis of this book. The hypothesis starts from some familiar facts, almost not worth stating. One fact is that human thoughts have some unique properties, apparently unprecedented in the animal world, some of which are centered on predication. The other fact is that human ontogeny itself is rather unique, even among higher primates, on account of such features as helplessness, prolonged immaturity, massive and lengthy adult dependence, intense psychological bonding, and a surprising capacity for assimilating language and culture. These unusual features force, and also guide, human children to develop their minds in unique directions and in particular to develop predicative thoughts.

What is paradoxical about this idea is that most of the mind-designing features of human ontogeny may have little, if anything, to do with thinking in general, yet they manage to steer the child's thinking in a direction unprecedented in evolution for its power and reach. I trust this is paradox enough. If it isn't, then consider also the other idea, pursued below, that key resources for predication—and also for mastering communicative meaning and word reference along the way—develop mostly out of dated and frequently transient skills, whose rationale and modus operandi respond essentially and often exclusively to specific as well as dated challenges of infancy and early childhood. Most of these initial skills are not even retained beyond childhood. Furthermore, these early challenges are mostly interpersonal and communicational, hence social, and the abilities that the child develops to handle them are decisively shaped at critical junctures by adult intervention and guidance, hence again socially. All this amounts to saying that the cognitive ability to think predicatively is assembled in contexts of social interaction out of a cocktail of disparate resources, most of which are not cognitive and usually not even internal to the child's mind, and whose rationale and functions are specific to and generated by unique as well as dated parameters of human ontogeny. Again, I trust this is paradox enough.

To understand this ontogenetic process and its denouement, it helps to remember that development is a slice and stage of evolution, with its own selection pressures and adaptive responses, and therefore that it should be analyzed in its own evolutionary terms. This evolutionary analysis matters, according to section 3.1, because many biological traits, including mental faculties, are the outcome of dated selective pressures and adaptive responses specific to particular stages of development. This is true of most of the pressures and adaptations that contribute to the child's abilities to mean, refer, and predicate. The evolutionary aspect of the mental development that leads to predication is perhaps best understood as an arms race between the child's teleology and the demands, challenges, and opportunities of adult culture. This arms race, discussed in section 3.2, explains how the child's manipulation of adults is exploited by the latter by constantly inserting and forcing the assimilation of linguistic, cultural, and behavioral innovations into the child's repertory of adaptations. Tracking the unfolding of this arms race, section 3.3 previews the central hypothesis of this book by proposing that the abilities to mean, refer, and predicate are assembled along an ontogenetic staircase, whose main steps involve mostly interpersonal and communicational interactions between children and adults. Section 3.4 introduces the idea, developed later in the book, that this ontogenetic staircase leads to a predicative redesign of the child's thinking.

3.1 Why Development

There are several reasons why human ontogeny appears to be an evolutionarily unique incubator of predicative thinking. Some reasons have already emerged as implications of the critical discussion of the previous chapter—in particular, the likely absence of the ability to predicate in animal and infant minds, and the possibility that far from being innate as a dedicated ability, predication may develop as a composite competence assembled out of disparate abilities that respond to challenges specific to early childhood. Even though the thematic categories of object, property, relation, and others, as well as the capacity to combine them in mental coinstantiations, may be viewed as prerequisites of predication, I see no evidence that the heart of predication—the topic-comment-presupposition format, and the intended directedness and descriptiveness—has verifiable animal or infant precursors. According to chapter 6, it is also possible that predication may have been absent in most of the hominid lineage as well. As a result, the ability to predicate might not be the outcome of a gradual *phylogenetic* evolution. Yet predication develops uniformly and is present in any normal human mind, so it cannot be the outcome of an inexplicable or random accident. Individual learning is not an option, either, as argued later. It is therefore plausible to conjecture that predication evolved out of various adaptations of human ontogeny, in response to its specific and unique challenges.

In order to understand the force of this conjecture, it is worth recalling another familiar but often forgotten fact—namely, that development itself *is* evolution. The reason is simple: selection works on phenotypes, not genotypes, and genotypes become phenotypes, in particular minds and bodies, during development. The work of selection forces is done through, during, and on development. Through and during development, because it is by means of developmental programs that the genome becomes expressed in a phenotype. How else would the genes be mapped into full organisms? Evolution also acts on development because in discharging its phenotype-building function, development generates its own pressures and adaptive responses to such pressures.

Many of these pressures and responses are local and dated. The responses can thus be regarded as *ontogenetic adaptations*. Survival and making it to the next stage are the most obvious and vital of pressures on the developing phenotype (Williams 1966, 44). The resulting adaptations impact on bodily and mental architectures, and create opportunities for further selective pressures and hence further adaptations. This is why developmental processes continue to bring additional ontogenetic adaptations on line until adulthood (Tooby and Cosmides 1992, 81). This is also why it can be plausibly said that what is selected for in evolution are ontogenetic trajectories rather than adult organisms (Bjorklund and Pellegrini 2000; Tomasello 1999). Several such convergent trajectories in human ontogeny gradually build the mental architecture for predication. The building process has some unique features—familiar yet again surprising in their consequences.

Human ontogeny is unusually long, immature, helpless, and massively adult dependent. There is one major reason for this: a premature birth due to the rapidly expanding size of the newborn's brain and skull, which continues to grow apace after birth as well. The human offspring thus enters the world and operates in it with an unfinished or not fully wired brain. As a result, for many years it is open to many interferences and challenges from the outside world. In particular, the interferences and challenges originating in the adult social and cultural environments generate tremendous pressures that further delay as well as complicate the eventual programming of the young brain. These pressures operate in the context of an arms race that drives the development of meaning, reference, and predication.

3.2 Two Evolutionary Games

The child's mental advance toward predication, through the mastery of communicative meaning and word reference, is driven and shaped by two evolutionary games: the child's adaptation game, and the adult initiation game, as we may call them. The child evolves a variety of adaptations to the surrounding physical, social, linguistic, and cultural worlds in order to stay well and make it to the next stage. At the same time, adult parenting practices evolved so as to turn these adaptations into opportunities to introduce the child to language and the ways of culture. The interaction of these two games takes the form of an arms race that eventually redesigns the child's mind in a predicative format of thinking and communicating.

The Arms Race

The well-being of the immature child depends vitally on adult assistance. To get that assistance, the child must figure out and successfully engage adults as well as their ways of dealing with the physical, social, linguistic, and cultural worlds. This is why it is of utmost importance for the child's mind to evolve effective strategies to connect and communicate with, as well as read or interpret, adult minds in order to get all the help from them, also exploit them, and understand and emulate the adult ways and means. The child's ontogenetic adaptations, directed at other minds through unique forms of communication and social interaction, will be those that play a vital role in the development of meaning, reference, and predication. For these reasons, I call these adaptations *interpersonal*.

To link up with the critical discussion of the last chapter, I note that despite the presence in many animal minds of such enabling resources as thematic categories of objects, properties, relations, and more, the attention that formats new-given information structures, the communicative signals that target definite states of affairs, and possibly the operation of a language of thought (in Fodor's sense), it is the lack of such interpersonal ontogenetic adaptations—more than the lack of a natural language—that most likely prevents animal minds from developing the abilities to mean, refer, and predicate.

It is the interpersonal adaptations that enable children to acquire bits and pieces of social, linguistic, and cultural knowledge. But as soon as they have done so, children are further pressured to build on these acquisitions, and develop still more sophisticated skills of communication with and understanding of adult minds, which in turn open new windows on more complex forms of social interaction, language and culture, and so on and so forth, until late adolescence and beyond. It is an intense and relentless arms race that leads to predication, abstract thinking, and eventually an intellect.

Three implications of this arms race are important for the present analysis. One is that the arms race explains why most of the child's mental resources involved in predication are dated acquisitions, on which other dated acquisitions are built, in an escalating spiral, and therefore why the resulting predication competence is essentially an outcome of the peculiarities of the human ontogeny. But according to the second implication, predication is not an endogenously driven outcome but rather a by-product of the child's interactions with and adaptations to adults and their culture. A third implication is that like all arms races, from biological to political and military, this one generates its own momentum and dynamics, whose effects cannot be explained outside its context. The effect that matters here is the redesign of the child's mind that results in predicative thinking. The why, when, and how of this redesign process are previewed in the next two sections.

3.3 Ontogenetic Staircase

A Developmental Hypothesis

The account of predication proposed in this book is made of a central hypothesis and a developmental story that elaborates and documents it in the chapters that follow. The hypothesis is that the child's ability to think and communicate in predicative terms grows out of her understanding of the referential acts of conventionally symbolic communication and (in particular) explicit naming in contexts of shared attention. *The child's grasp of the explicitly and socially intended word reference—or coreference, as I will call it—becomes the mental incubator and template of predication.*

This hypothesis does *not* entail that all or most words are acquired through explicit naming by adults in contexts of shared attention. Many and perhaps most words are not so acquired. The child's first words are certainly not acquired in this way (Bates 1976; P. Bloom 2000). Animals, from parrots to dogs, learn words but not by explicit naming based on shared attention. My hypothesis is that by redesigning, within language, an earlier prelinguistic format of communication by joint comments on shared topics, the explicit naming by adults generates in the child's mind schemes that become a template for predication. The child's first words, as well as the words learned by sundry species of animals, involve *other* mechanisms—such as association, mimicking, reading behavioral clues, and so on—which do *not* generate an explicit and socially shared sense of word coreference, and therefore do not lead to predication. In short, my hypothesis is about *only one* mechanism of acquiring words, but that is *the* mechanism that is crucial to the development of predication.

Like all biological traits, the ability to predicate is an outcome of development. But unlike most biological traits, this ability grows out of the convergence of diverse developments, often unrelated to the final result, and does so for reasons that are mostly developmental. As ontogenetic adaptations, those diverse developments in turn create opportunities for still other developments, and other adaptive abilities, whence the metaphor of an ontogenetic staircase that is *assembled*—rather than endogenously matured or else individually learned—in an arms race between the child's adaptation game and the adult initiation game. Echoing the earlier critique of animal or perceptual predication, my hypothesis implies that the child's predicative thoughts are formed *first* in contexts of communication, and for reasons of communication, rather than in dealings with physical objects and their properties, or in the mere exercise of perception and attention.

What I propose to do next is introduce the main ontogenetic steps to predication, so that the reader can have a preview of the developmental process. I will provide only brief summaries of what happens at each step, and leave for the next chapters the task of elaborating and empirically documenting their specific contributions to the assembly of predication. So here we go.

The Steps

From the ground level of immaturity and helplessness, the first step up on the ontogenetic staircase to predication is that of infant-adult physiological coregulation.

Step 1: Coregulation
immaturity and helplessness → infant-adult coregulation

The newborn is not a complete and self-sufficient biological system. Therefore, it needs adult assistance and regulative involvement. As the infant grows and adults get busier with their own affairs, the proximal physiological coregulation is gradually replaced by a *psychological* coregulation at a distance, carried out in terms of exchanges of looks, facial expressions, gestures, and other behaviors that convey—and are intended to do so—inner or mental states, in the early stages mostly in the form of emotions and affective expressions. The psychological coregulation at a distance becomes a new form of *communication*—at first, bilateral, spontaneous, and unconventionalized. Thus:

Step 2: Intersubjective communication
physiological coregulation → psychological coregulation at a distance → bilateral intersubjective communication → the child's recognition of the adult's child-directed mental intent and a mutual acknowledgment of this recognition

This form of communication reveals to the child the *mental intent* expressed by the adult's communicative acts. The child recognizes that the adult's intent is to direct communicative meanings at the child, and have the child recognize this intent. This is what makes the communication *intersubjective*. It lays the foundation for the child's later recognition of the adult's *coreferential* intent to get the child to understand gestures, conventional symbols, and words as referring to shared targets in the world. This later recognition becomes the platform for predication.

The child's advance from recognizing an adult's bilateral mental intent to recognizing an adult's coreferential intent goes through a *trilateral* or *world-shared* communication. Its first form is imperative, in that it is intended by the child to attract and influence an adult's attention; egocentric, in that it is represented only from the standpoint of the child; and unilateral, in that the coreferential intent of the other is not yet recognized. This new form of communication, often called *protodeclarative*, marks a further step on the ontogenetic staircase to predication:

Step 3: Protodeclarative communication
getting and maintaining the adult's attention by relating to external targets = protodeclarative communication → unilateral and egocentric child-world-adult triangulation

Sometime around nine to twelve months, the child seems to assemble and blend the two communication tracks—coregulative and imperative—

into *joint triangulations* of targets. In so doing, the child seems to insert the earlier bilateral recognition of the adult's mental intent into the protodeclarative child-world-adult triangulation. The result is:

Step 4: Joint triangulations
joint triangulations → connect bilateral intersubjective communication with protodeclarative child-world-adult triangulations

Unlike joint triangulations, whose mental coordination is still shaky, and whose reach is proximal and vague, the next step of shared attention coordinates the perspectives and world-directed relations around a precise distal target as a shared topic. Shared attention is a topic fixer because it enables the child to grasp the *coreferential intent* implicit in the adult's communicative acts.

Step 5: Shared coreference
intersubjective protodeclarative communication + shared attention → topic fixation → recognition of coreferential intent → shared coreference

By managing a mutually acknowledged coreferential intent, shared attention enables the child to use a gesture or vocalization toward the adult in the same way that the adult uses it toward the child—the so-called role reversal imitation (Tomasello 2003, 27). As a result, drawing on earlier exposure to the ritualized character of many adult gestures and vocalizations, the child begins to understand the arbitrary or *symbolic* and *conventional* character of adult communication. Hence:

Step 6: Understanding conventional symbols
shared attention → mutual recognition of coreferential intent + role reversal imitation → understanding conventionally symbolic acts of coreference

The ground is now ready for the next and crucial step. This is the child's understanding of words acquired by explicit naming in contexts of shared attention—or *shared naming,* as I will call it—as directing attention to a target as a topic in order to elicit comments about it. Therefore:

Step 7: Sense of word coreference
grasp of words as conventional symbols + shared attention + recognition of coreferential intent → representing words introduced by shared naming as directing attention to a shared target as a topic open to still-nonverbal comments = the first sense of word coreference

Having mastered shared naming, the child also realizes that words can be used to make comments about already-named shared topics. Like all comments encountered so far in contexts of shared attention, the commenting words of the adult are likely to be registered by the child as intended to relate jointly to some aspect of the previously fixed referent. Thus:

Step 8: Comments on topics by way of words
mastery of words introduced by shared naming → words fixing a topic as referent ← at which aspects (e.g., property, relation, action, or event) are directed by further words operating as comments

The child's mental road to predication is now open. For suppose that "A" is a topic-fixing word in a context of shared attention, or situated context, and "B" is an aspect-selecting commenting word. Then, step 8 enables the child initially to schematize situated or perceptually grounded predications of the linguistic form "A is B" in the following format:

Step 9: Situated predication
the adult's comment directs the child to attend to some aspect B of A's referent; and the child reciprocates in the same way

When words are mastered and used by the child in contexts that are unsituated or nonperceptual, and often unshared with adults, as suggested by

Step 10: Unsituated predication
mastery of unsituated words → fixing topics as referents ← at which aspects (property, relation, action, or event) are directed through further commenting words

Then the child is ready and able to schematize the unsituated and adult-independent linguistic predication "A is B" according to the following template:

Step 11: Predication simpliciter
presupposing a context of thinking or communication, aspect B as meaning of a predicate is intently selected, encoded, and directed, as comment, at the subject A's referent, as topic [the P-dimensions], in order to represent and inform about a conceptually structured fact as predicative proposition [S-dimensions]

We have here the mental matrix of predication with its most important P-dimensions—the intended comment (or predicate-)to-topic (or subject) directedness and the topic-comment-presupposition format rolled into one, and the intended descriptiveness of the resulting structure. The task of the rest of this book is to explain how this last step develops out of the preceding ones along the ontogenetic staircase just outlined, and also to explain how, along the way, the child's imperative mind is redesigned into one capable of propositional thinking of the predicative sort. The story of this redesign is previewed next.

3.4 Mental Redesign

Young children are goal-driven, pragmatic organisms, mostly sensorimotor in cognition and imperative in their early communication. Like their animal precursors, young children want things and engage in actions that will satisfy what they want. In their social interactions and communications with adults, young children want things from adults, pressure them into doing things, signal various desires and other internal states, and give adults orders or make demands on them. The instrumental thoughts of young children are therefore likely to have a *how-to* format, perhaps best represented as *if [input is such and such], then [do such and so].* The children's imperative acts of communication, including early word use, are much like actions directed at adults (Bates 1976). So far, so animal; nothing in this picture presages predicative thinking. And yet, in a few years, the same children will be able to think and communicate descriptively and predicatively. How can one explain this metamorphosis?

Learning is one option. But learning in what domain? Since actions on and perceptions of the physical environment would not guide the child toward predication, as already noted in the animal case, the domain must be social and in particular communication with adults. The problem is that the young child's communication is imperative and likely to absorb new information in its *existing* format. The adult's communicational responses are deliberately geared to what the child can assimilate, in the form of baby talk or motherese, helpful gestures, and facial expressions, and rarely display the declarative format of normal adult conversation. And even if the young child were exposed to normal adult conversation, it is hard to see with what resources—and for what reasons—the child would recognize and extract the predicative format out of the flow of adult speech.

If, as Bates (1976) argues, the capacity for predication is undedicated, and builds on attention and its role in separating new from given information, then (as argued already) it fails to handle the topic-comment format and the intentful directedness of predication. And since perceptual attention develops quite early, why does it take until around the age of two or so for predication to show up in the child's communication? But if the alleged innate capacity for predication is dedicated and has its specific domain, as many authors assume, but takes its time to mature, what would explain its presence in the human genome? In particular, what would explain the intentful directedness, descriptiveness, and topic-comment-presupposition dimensions of predication? Innate are likely to be some enabling resources such as the naive-physical categories of object, property, or relation, the naive-biological categories of agent and action, the capacities for attention and perhaps forming thematic coinstantiations, and the syntactic formalism of a mental or natural language—all necessary, but shown earlier not to be sufficient for predication.

Perhaps the most cogent evidence against the innateness of a specialized capacity for predication as well as against learning to predicate is that the ontogenesis of predication seems to advance in a rather tight and well-scheduled lockstep with the ontogenesis of several other *disparate* abilities that, jointly, could actually explain the emergence of the P-dimensions of predication. The coincidence is too striking to be accidental, as I propose to show in the next chapters.

The explanation I propose of why and how the child's instrumental cognition turns descriptive, and her imperative communication turns declarative is one of an *assembly* of new mental abilities out of a variety of precursor abilities—a process that is fueled by the arms race noted earlier. As the young child strives to do well and manage her goal-directed actions as well as imperative communications with adult assistance, the adult initiation of the child into language and culture increasingly forces the child's interpersonal adaptations to assimilate novelties, insert them as components into her existing goal strategies, and integrate them in prior components. The adult initiation policies introduce innovations that once inserted and assembled by the child's mind into its instrumental and imperative modes of thinking and communication, generate mental schemes that gradually redesign from inside the child's thinking in a predicative format.

How would this redesign-by-assembly process work? The guiding idea is this. Young children get adult coregulation and help, and also use adults as a means to their goals, most often by way of communication. To achieve these ends, children develop mental schemes that enable them to represent and manipulate the communication-relevant relations that adults have to the children and the world around them. These mental schemes, which represent child-adult (bilateral) relations, adult-world relations, and child-adult-world (triangular) relations, gradually generate a template for the predication competence. Since communication is not only comprehension but also production, and therefore involves communicative *thoughts* about what to convey intently and later explicitly say to adults, the eventual effect of the developments along the ontogenetic staircase will be to redesign the child's *communicative thoughts* in a predicative direction.

The most critical step in this redesign process occurs at step 7 on the ontogenetic staircase, when the child first acquires a sense of word coreference. The mental scheme that represents word coreference has descriptive and normative force, as the child begins to realize that it is an obligatory fact that words refer to something specific, and that one can be right or wrong about the reference relation. The other two critical dimensions of predication—the intentful predicate-to-subject directedness and the topic-comment-presupposition format—emerge as the child becomes able, in the next few steps on the ontogenetic staircase, to recast shared triangulations in entirely linguistic terms.

Predication thus develops *within* the imperative envelope of child-adult communication. The predicative redesign of the child's communicative thinking is caused by the new mental tools acquired through word learning, still used for a while for imperative and instrumental reasons, but with increased sensitivity to the descriptive force of words and the way they reformat the comment-to-topic relation. This continuity through change can explain the incremental transition to predicative thinking exemplified by the ontogenetic staircase. It can also explain the fact that the work of predication ends up being routinized, abbreviated, and spontaneous, as does in general the how-to or know-how work of conation and cognition, from sensorimotor to thinking. Predication therefore becomes second nature. How this comes about and why is what the remainder of this book attempts to explain in more detail.

4 Roots

The story of predication begins with two central puzzles. One is the puzzle of the intended comment-to-topic directedness: the intent to communicate something about something else. The other is the puzzle of intended descriptiveness: using the comment-to-topic directedness to state a fact, describe a situation, or share information. These accomplishments are puzzling because young human children begin their lives as goal-driven organisms, whose cognition is sensorimotor and instrumental or practical, and whose communication is imperative and dedicated mostly to signaling. And yet, sometime between the ages of two and three, children begin to engage in different and novel forms of communication and thinking. The communication is mostly symbolic, and through it situations and actions are acknowledged, points of interest and experiences are shared—first gesturally and then verbally—new facts and activities are learned through description and explicit instruction, and stories are told, often without any immediate behavioral utility. In handling this new form of communication, both at its production and comprehension ends, the child's thoughts themselves turn into mental structures that deliberately describe facts and situations by commenting on topics.

How can one explain this puzzling transition? My answer will come in two major parts. The first part, told in this chapter, is about the ingredients that go into the final product. These ingredients form the developmental roots of predication. These are ontogenetic abilities and predispositions that, adapted to as well as redesigned in interpersonal and communicational interactions with adults, end up organizing the child's predicative thinking. Temporally, this chapter covers infancy and early childhood, without assigning specific dates to the various developments to be discussed. The second part of my answer, told in the next chapter, is about the actual developmental recipe that, in its more precise and dated temporal unfolding, assembles the ingredients into a mental capacity to predicate in thinking and communication.

I distinguish three major roots of predication. The first, examined in section 4.1, is the mutual or coregulative physiological and then psychological interaction between infant and adult, due to the infant's biological immaturity and helplessness, which generates a bilateral and intersubjective communication by mental sharing, mostly of an affective nature. The second root, discussed in section 4.2, is the young child's parallel imperative and world-bound communication that treats adults as a means to her goals, thus creating the opportunity for adult interference and mental redesign. This opportunity, according to section 4.3, is immensely helped by a third root, which is the child's emerging sense of other minds—a sense that builds mostly on and blends the bilateral mental sharing of infancy along with a growing naive psychology.

As abilities and dispositions, these roots of predication reflect the vital priorities of young children, their adaptation game—securing adult coregulation through bilateral communication, reaching their basic goals such as food, protection, attention, play, relief from pain, and so on, through imperative communication, and developing a sense of the adults' relations to the world and the children themselves. As the next chapter argues, these roots become tools in the adults' initiation game of exploiting the parameters of the child's first priority (regulation through communication) in order to interfere in and guide the second priority (achieving basic goals through imperative communication) so as to force the child to assimilate adult language and culture. Since the child's coregulative and imperative forms of communication directed at adults involve communicative thoughts, the eventual effect of adult interference and guidance will be to reshape the child's communicative thoughts in a predicative format.

4.1 Coregulative Communication

The story is familiar from a large and diverse body of recent work (Adamson 1995; Bjorklund 2000; Bates 1976; Bruner 1983; Hobson 1993; Tomasello 1999; Trevarthen 1993; Werner and Kaplan 1963; also Bogdan 1997, 2000, 2001). My reading of this literature, on which I will frequently draw in this chapter without much further citation, and which underlies the main argument of this section, is that the coregulative interaction between child and adult contains the basic elements of meaning-conveying communication, which is *the* key contributor to predication. Most of these basic elements have a physiological basis and origin.

Inside the womb, the human fetus is part of the biological system of the mother. Outside the womb, the infant becomes self-regulating in many but not all respects. Since the infant is an incomplete system, and in particular an incomplete and imperfect regulatory self, some of the regulatory tasks, especially the homeostatic ones, are taken over by the mother. To some extent, this is a more general mammalian and certainly primate predicament. What seems uniquely human about it are several aspects that turn out to be essential to the ontogenesis of communication and (later) predication.

Psychological Turn

As the infant grows and adults get busier with their own affairs, the proximal physiological coregulation is gradually replaced by a spatially distant *psychological* coregulation by way of exchanges of looks, facial expressions, smiles, gestures, and other behaviors that convey—and are meant to convey—mostly emotions and other affective states.

There are two readings of this story. The lean one sees the exchanges of expressions of feelings and emotions as no more than another form of physiological coregulation by psychological means, but lacking communicative intentions on the part of the infant (Bermudez 1998, 254). On a richer reading, the psychological coregulation ushers in a prelinguistic communication between infants and adults—a protoconversation in a give-and-take, address-and-reply manner (Bruner 1983; Hobson 1993; Trevarthen 1993). Although not communicating about anything outside the interaction and certainly not about the world—a protoconversation without a topic, so to speak—the infant nevertheless is intent on conveying affective experiences to the adult and in turn acknowledges the adult's experiences.

It may not be easy to adjudicate this debate, or in general accept the notion that communication can be just bilateral and without a topic. What I find important, on either reading, is that the sustained bilateral exchanges enable the infant to develop several abilities that will be essential to the ontogenesis of communication, word acquisition, and predication. Here is a succinct list.

Synchronization One such ability is the *synchronization* of physiological exchanges between the infant and the mother, bearing on their heart rhythms, thermoregulation, autonomic regulation, biological clocks, and so on. The result is that the infant can anticipate the mother's rhythms and reactions, and adjust his behaviors accordingly, thereby coordinating his behaviors with the mother's, and resonating to the changes in the motherly and generally adult behavior (Feldman, Mayes, and Swain 2005;

Trevarthen 1993). This physiological adaptation turns out to be decisive for infant-adult communication, to the extent that the infant's fine coordination with and sensitivity to adult physiology and behavior will be transferred, on a psychological plane, to the communicative signals later exchanged with adults.

Bilateral Mental Sharing Synchronized physiological exchanges underpin those exchanges of experiences that are not only shared but also whose sharing is mutually recognized and acknowledged. Each partner is aware that the other has recognized the exchange. For example, by smiling and being smiled at, and repeating the cycle with variations that are in turn acknowledged, the infant becomes aware that the other recognizes and reacts not only to the infant's smiling but to the sharing itself as well. This mutual recognition of what is mentally shared forms an indispensable platform of human communication. When child-adult communication turns toward the world, becoming trilateral, this sense of sharedness will also extend to the worldly topics of communication and the surrounding context.

Intersubjective Communication A synchronized and shared psychological coregulation at a distance generates a form of intersubjective communication that is attuned to and in sync with the behavioral expressions of the earlier physiological exchanges. Both infants and adults are clearly primed, ready, able, and pleased to engage in it. In its early stages, the communication that results from psychological coregulation by mental sharing is exclusively bilateral and lacks immediate world-directed import. Many animals address messages, such as bodily signals or emotions, to conspecifics and members of other species. Primates also evolved eye-to-eye contact (Gomez 1998, 2005). But such bilateral communication among animals is generally intended to signal the communicator's future behavior (for instance, aggression or reconciliation) and thus affect the addressee's behavior. The infant-adult intersubjective communication is biologically utilitarian, in that it secures coregulation and expresses internal conditions, but is not always specifically aimed at some immediate behavioral effect or specific target in the world. Such freedom from utilitarian effects and targets may later mean flexibility in expressing attitudes and comments about a rich variety of topics, and in understanding words as referring to a rich variety of targets. This flexibility will turn out to be essential to the child's mastery of predication.

Coordination and Reciprocity The earlier physiological synchronization and the resulting mental sharing of experiences ensure that the early intersubjective communication between infant and adult is coordinated and reciprocal. Having studied the phenomenon of infant-adult coordination extensively and in great empirical detail, Colwyn Trevarthen (1993, 126) concludes that the human infant is an interpersonal self who "possesses motives that detect complementary motives in others and require the response of others; it is the core, transmodal features of motivation, coded as emotions, and transferred from subject to subject in this form, that permit the intercoordination of psychological states between subjects." Trevarthen construes *motives* as mental functions that cause and direct movements and psychological reactions. This notion of motive is rather close to the notion of intent that I am using in this book.

This reciprocal and synchronized coordination of motives or intents, coded as emotions and feelings, and expressed in looks, facial patterns, and gestures, enables the coregulative communication between child and adult to take the form of a protoconversation in a give-and-take, address-and-reply, taking-turns manner. At this stage it is a preverbal form of conversation without a topic, a series of reciprocated responses, but it has the virtue of anticipating the format of—and thus creating the matrix for—later verbal communication (Adamson 1995; Bruner 1983; Hobson 1993).

The Emergence of Comments At this point I venture the conjecture that so construed, the motives or intents of infants and adults, expressed in their coregulative interactions, seem to begin to function as a sort of bilateral *comments* addressed to each other along two tracks: on the one hand, the child's imperative and egocentric expression of goals, impulses, wants, or other inner states; and on the other hand, an other-centered expression of affect, interest, curiosity, and other forms of interpersonal relatedness. This dual-track nature of motives or intents, expressed as comments, suggests that a *comment can be construed as an expression of intent to produce in a partner a mental effect (egocentric track), which intent is recognized by the partner (interpersonal track)*. The reader will notice here an anticipation of the Gricean-style analysis of meaning-conveying communication. Construed along these lines, the coregulative comment becomes a basic contributor to meaning-conveying communication and later predication.

A First, Bilateral Sense of Other Minds

Intersubjective communication appears to enable children to begin to discern the mental subtext and directedness of another person's looks, smiles, gestures, vocalizations, and other expressions of bilateral comments. By *mental subtext* I mean different inner states or conditions, such as emotions, feelings, attention, and their various kinds (happiness, sorrow, pain, visual focus and intensity, and so on), expressed outwardly in facial expressions, gestures, expressions of the eyes, bodily movements, postures, and actions. By *mental directedness* I mean the property of emotions, attention, cognitive and conative states, and particularly motives or intents, outwardly expressed, to relate to and focus on different targets—other people first, then external things and situations. In early bilateral communication, the first target of the adult's mental directedness, which the child recognizes and acknowledges, is the child himself. It is a I-You and You-Me sort of mental directedness, which is not yet the world directedness of the mental states registered later by the child's naive psychology but instead is a critical premise of the latter (Bogdan 2000; Gomez 2005; Hobson 1993; Tomasello et al. 2005).

There are at least two ways to explain this incipient bilateral and intersubjective *sense of the mental in others*, as we may call it. It is a sense of the subtext *and* directedness of other minds. One explanation is that the protracted communicational exchanges with adults enable young children to discern and project in others a sort of invariant patterns behind the variety of their outward expressions and behaviors. These invariant patterns define the *mental* (or rather what counts as mental) for the child in coregulative and communicational terms, for exclusively coregulative and communicational reasons. The emphasis here is on the fact that the young child resonates to and understands other minds *to the extent*—and *only* to the extent—that the child registers invariants behind their overt manifestations, and reciprocates, acts on, and reacts to these manifestations in light of the invariants they express.

Another plausible explanation could be that young children map the observed features of adult facial expressions and behaviors onto their own internal experiences (emotions and feelings) and motor intentions (Gopnik and Meltzoff 1997). Such mapping generates a sort of "like-me" equivalence that joins outward expressions of other people with one's own internal conditions. As an innate ability that operates immediately after birth, imitation (another bilateral exercise) is well positioned to produce and reinforce such like-me equivalencies and therefore bring about a self-based sense of the mental in others.

Whatever the right explanation, and there could be others as well, the young child's initial and bilateral sense of the mental in others, construed as sensitivity to the mental subtext and bilateral me-directedness of other people, turns out to be a potent ontogenetic adaptation to mutual psychological regulation at a distance, through bilateral and later trilateral communication.

It is worth emphasizing that this initial sense of the mental in others is probably *not* the outcome of a naive psychology. I noted in the previous chapter that I construe naive psychology (or the naive theory of mind) as having the primary function of registering and representing another mind's *relations* to the world (Bogdan 1997). Intersubjective communication is not yet about mind-world relations; it is about *bilateral* coregulation by psychological means. In support of this position, it can be observed that other primate species have a sophisticated social cognition and perhaps even rudiments of naive psychology, and yet for all we know, they do not have an intuitive sense of other minds, particularly their subtext and directedness (but for a different view, see Gomez 2005). Furthermore, autistic people are generally good at registering other people's visible relations to the world, such as seeing or gesturing, but are less good at grasping complex and less visible mental states, such as emotions, beliefs, and intentions. According to accounts that I find plausible, this is largely because autistic children are initially deficient in intersubjective coregulation and bilateral communication (Hobson 1993). Nevertheless, as mentioned later in this chapter, there are good reasons to think that naive psychology, which kicks in later in early childhood, ends up integrating the child's initial sense of the mental-in-others into its own conceptual gadgetry.

A Bilateral Sense of Communicative Meaning

The developments noted so far enable the young child to engage in meaning-based communication—a milestone in the ontogenetic construction of predication. Animal communication is about signaling and registering one's internal condition, behavioral readiness, or some event in the world. Although it does all these things, human communication is also, and essentially, in the business of conveying and registering the meanings of communicative acts. *Communicative meaning* is construed here as a function of what people intend to express or convey in a mutually acknowledged manner. This construal was insightfully anticipated by Mead (1910, 1934) at the turn of the twentieth century [see note on Mead]. Several decades later, Grice (1957) famously explicated it. Grice's analysis grounds a sense of meaning in a sense of the mental, which I—not Grice—construe in terms of mental subtext and bilateral directedness, as explained a few paragraphs ago. In developmental terms—again, not Grice's—children first understand meaning in bilateral exchanges of mutually expressed experiences before understanding it in a linguistic triangle with an adult and a shared world. Predicative thoughts, I will suggest, are designed along this progression in the child's understanding and use of meaningful communicative acts.

To put this idea in a more definitional form, I group facial expressions, bodily postures, actions, gestures, pointings, looks, gazes, vocalizations, and spoken utterances under the generic notion of *communicative acts*, henceforth (simply) acts. On Grice's classical account of meaning (1957),

- *acts mean* something because communicators mean something; and
- *communicators mean* something by an act if and only if they intend the act to produce some mental effect—such as attention, sympathy, emotion, or belief—in an audience by means of the audience's recognition of this intent (to produce the mental effect in question)

So far, the child-adult bilateral communication is meaningful, yet nonreferential, by conveying to an audience a mental state of the communicator, and nothing more. The intent of a communicative act is exclusively other directed. The communicative act means something by expressing a mental state (such as happiness or worry) because (say) mother means it this way; and mother means the act this way because she intends the act, as an expression of a mental condition, to produce an effect in the child (say, an emotional reaction) by having the child recognize this intent. And lo and behold, the child does recognize the intent by producing an emotional response, in the guise of a happy smile and some gestures, which the mother in turn recognizes as the child's recognition of her intent. The communication loop is thus closed bilaterally. The other-directed meaning it conveys is now captured by a mutually recognized mental sharing [see note on Grice Read Developmentally].

Transition

Summing up so far, coregulative communication begins at birth, first physiologically, and then increasingly psychologically, intersubjectively but only bilaterally. Its main predication-promising acquisitions in the first nine months or so are a synchronized sense of coordination and sharing of experiences in communication, which grounds a sense of the subtext and bilateral directedness of other minds—what I called "a sense of the mental in others." The latter in turn enables the child to form a sense of the bilateral meanings of communicative acts. I use the vague concept of *sense of* in order to leave open to empirical research the determination of the mechanisms by means of which young children grasp and represent all these predication-building acquisitions.

During the same regulative period, and later, the child is also, and as vitally, an agent pursuing goals in the outside world. This basic fact is reflected on the parallel imperative track of child communication, to which I turn next. The imperative track is equally essential to the development of predicative thoughts because it first implements the world-bound teleology of the young child, and governs the production part of her communication and thinking. Once under the child's control, imperative communication and particularly its production part will face adult pressures to adopt, assimilate, and use the sense of meaning along with the other predication-enabling acquisitions of coregulative communication and their subsequent developments.

4.2 Imperative Communication

The Child as Agent

Since birth, the young child is an inveterate imperative communicator who signals to adults not only internal conditions but also outside goals, and makes demands on them to attend to those conditions and reach those goals. The child's imperative acts of communication are much like actions directed at adults—behavioral ways of causing adults to do things desired by the child. There are many accounts of child communication, but when it comes to goal-directed actions, physical or communicative, and their impact on mental development, the most far-probing and comprehensive theoretical framework remains that initiated by Jean Piaget and his school. To my knowledge, perhaps the best Piagetian account of communication as goal-directed behavior is that of Elizabeth Bates (1976, 1979) and her collaborators. It is a sophisticated, complex, and interdisciplinary account, with a keen sense of the biological and teleological parameters of the child's communication and acquisition of language. So without much further citation, I will take Bates's work and that of some precursors (particularly Greenfield and Smith 1976) that she relies on as guides for my inquiry into the child's imperative communication.

Although by itself imperative communication is unlikely to turn declarative and predicative, as the history of animal communication shows, its human version seems to offer opportunities for a such a shift when at least three conditions are met: the child attends to and uses targets in the world to obtain as well as maintain the adult's attention, interest, and cooperation (the so-called protodeclarative communication); the adult pressures the child to recruit the abilities of coregulative communication, particularly exchanges of meaning-conveying comments (in the Gricean sense), in order to meet the first condition; and when these two conditions are met, the adult inserts words—and the child begins to treats them—as tools intended to direct an interlocutor's attention to targets of shared interest as topics open to comments. Because the child is an agent intent on relating to adults and reaching her goals with adult help, and because imperative communication is world bound and thus trilateral, the child is likely to develop mental schemes that can effectively deal with the three conditions just noted. This is the developmental path I propose to map out in this section and the next chapter. It is the path that leads to meaningful communication about the world, reference and word acquisition, and predication.

The child's earliest imperative communication is mostly instinctive. Around nine months or so, its character changes dramatically in several key respects (Bates 1976, 34–38). The child begins to alternate her gaze between outside objects or events and the adult. This is evidence that the adult begins to play a role in the child's goal strategies, especially communicative ones. Similar evidence is to be found in the fact that the child now seems to adjust her communicative signals not only to her goals and the external contexts but also to how adults relate to the child's goals. (These two phenomena anticipate joint triangulations, a topic of the next chapter.) At about the same time, the child's communicative signals directed at adults also get abbreviated and ritualized, suggesting an emerging grasp of the conventional side of (still-preverbal) communication.

All these developments indicate an imperative communication that is becoming voluntary and deliberate. They also suggest that adults become deliberate targets as social tools in the child's goal-pursuing communication. Bates (1976, 51) distinguishes two strategies that the child employs in her imperative communication:

- *Protoimperative* Using adults as a means to nonsocial goals, such as reaching objects, influencing events, and so on
- *Protodeclarative* Using nonsocial means, such as giving, pointing to, and showing objects, as a means to obtain adult attention and participation; importantly, a protodeclarative is a preverbal attempt of the child to attract

the adult's attention by *directing* it toward some event or object in the world

Protodeclarative communication alone can open the way to declarative communication and predicative thinking, when, replacing pointings to and showing objects, words and utterances are inserted as a new version of the imperative scheme <action/later word directed at object → get the adult's attention>. Not being aimed at the adult's attention, the other, protoimperative scheme <act physically on adult → get nonsocial goal> does not lend itself to this words-instead-of-actions substitution. To act on and influence an adult *at a distance*, the child must first aim to catch and direct the adult's attention to something in the world. Being directly and behaviorally aimed at the adult, protoimperative communication cannot do that. This fact alone might (just might) explain the absence of language and predication in nonhuman animals, given that their communication is at best protoimperative (using conspecifics to attain goals or signaling events) and aimed at influencing conspecific behavior. So the focus from now on will be exclusively on the *protodeclarative* version of imperative communication.

Protodeclaratives

Protodeclarative communication is imperative (whence the "proto" qualifier), insofar as the child acts communicatively to cause a mental state of attention in the adult and direct it toward some goal. It is also a procedural and sensorimotor form of communication, of the know-how sort, insofar as it involves the behavioral skills of acting communicatively on adults, through sounds and gestures, and thus causing them to do things. It is only later and gradually that words and utterances with referential value are inserted in the same imperative format, and for a while treated as sensorimotor actions, before the imperative format itself morphs into a declarative one.

According to Bates (1976, 57–63), as the adult becomes increasingly distant spatially, the child's physical contact with adults is replaced by calling the adult's attention to external objects. Both in early coregulative communication and later in protodeclarative communication, the spatial distancing of the adult forces the child to develop new communicative strategies that are no longer guided by her sensorimotor schemes of physical contact. The communicative means to secure adult attention and help become externalized as gestures and vocalizations operating as tools with psychological function and reach.

The new protodeclarative acts are directed at the adult by way of being directed at items in the world. Thus begins the unprecedented game of *child-world-adult triangulation*—another crucial step in the child's mental journey to predication. In its early stages (showing, giving, and pointing to objects), the triangulation involves an alternance of the child's gazes to the adult, then the targeted object, then the adult again, and so on. This is a sequential but uncoordinated and unshared triangulation, in that it has not yet incorporated the bilateral mental sharing, the sense of the other's mental intent as well as the mutual knowledge of the sharing and the intent, which all emerged on the parallel coregulative track of the child communication. By itself, unshared and uncoordinated triangulation through alternance of gazes, which apes also appear able to manage (Tomasello and Call 1997), is unlikely to lead to meaning-conveying communication, word acquisition, and hence predication.

In human children approaching their first anniversary, the regulative and protodeclarative forms of communication appear to join forces, generating mentally shared and increasingly coordinated triangulations of objects and events in the world, thereby preparing the ground for word acquisition and the mastery of predication. This will be the story of the next chapter. The main stimulus and shaper of these next steps on the ontogenetic staircase to predication is another vital root of predication, which is the child's sense of other minds. This is my next topic.

4.3 A Sense of Other Minds

The sense of other minds enables the child to register and respond first to the meaning-conveying bilateral intent in coregulative communication, and later to the referential intent in declarative and world-bound communication. (A reminder: I use the concept of "sense of the mental in others" or "sense of other minds" liberally in order to allow for a variety of mechanisms that may enable children and adults to grasp and represent the mental states of others.) In this section, I introduce and explicate the key resources of the child's sense of other minds, leaving for the next chapter the task of conjecturing how their contribution to predication may actually unfold ontogenetically.

The Clusters

Based on current evidence, the human sense of other minds appears to be assembled out of *three* distinct but eventually integrated clusters of abilities, initially operating in different domains and having different functions.

A first cluster, already familiar from the earlier discussion of coregulative communication in section 4.1 above, comprises abilities that operate from mind to mind, or bilaterally, and register the overt signs of the inner conditions of another mind, be they emotions, feelings, motives, or intents. These abilities register *mind-to-mind* relations and thus enable one to engage in *mental sharing*, as we may call it. These abilities were earlier said to be the ones that first make manifest the bilateral mental intent of someone's communicative acts.

Another candidate cluster comprises abilities that echo or mirror in one mind the actions of another individual. A recent discovery established that the same neurons fire when an individual acts in some way or watches another individual acting in same way. These neurons, aptly called *mirror neurons*, detected in humans and other primates (Rizzolatti et al. 1996), provide *action-mirroring* abilities. The understanding of these remarkable abilities is a work in progress, but there are already good reasons to think that they are involved in behavioral imitation, the learning of cultural practices and behavioral routines, and possibly, by analogy to self, reading the mental intent and direction of mirrored actions. Furthermore, if we construe the child's initial understanding of referring in terms of target-directed actions, such as pointing, then the action-mirroring abilities may assist the mind-to-mind abilities in registering somebody's referential intent. Finally, the action-mirroring abilities may also be involved in what Tomasello (2003) calls role-reversal imitation, which will be shown later to be essential to word acquisition.

This second cluster may also include the abilities to empathize with and simulate the mental states of another person. These abilities may actually draw on and reinforce mind-to-mind resources, from the first cluster, and also draw on emotion and affect mirroring capabilities, somewhat similar to those that mirror actions. (People do spontaneously feel sadness when they see others sad; laughter and yawning are spontaneously contagious; and so on.) The idea here is that the first two clusters produce not just bilateral information about but also a sort of mutual adjustment to, and often coordination of, mental states (mostly intents, emotions, and affects) and actions. These two clusters seem to be in place before, and thus provide a platform and matrix for, the development of a third cluster.

This third, more familiar, and more intensely studied cluster of abilities belongs to the child's naive psychology or naive theory of mind, whose primary function is to represent and interpret *mind-to-world relations*, such as seeing, desiring, and believing. According to the distinction introduced in chapter 2, section 2.4, this early naive psychology turns in later childhood into a more sophisticated and culturally sensitive folk or commonsense psychology. But this development is beyond the scope of my inquiry, which encompasses only the first three years of childhood (but see Bogdan 1997).

There are good reasons to think that the young child's naive psychology itself is under considerable pressure to coordinate, assemble, and integrate the abilities from the first two clusters into composite categories and schemes of an enriched naive psychology, capable of detecting and representing *both* the mental intent (and also affects and emotions) and the world relatedness of the communications and actions of other people. One such composite category, examined next, turns out to be vital to the development of word acquisition and predication.

The Two Faces of Intentionality

The academic vocabulary harbors two notions of intentionality. One notion, close to the *ordinary* usage, and also employed by most psychologists and neuroscientists, construes intentionality as having a goal or an intention to reach a goal, or acting with an intention to reach a goal. Setting aside, but only for a while, the difference between having a goal (usually an external state of affairs) and having a desire or intention (a mental state about a goal), I propose to accommodate the two readings under the notion of *purposefulness*.

The other notion of intentionality is *philosophical*. It construes intentionality as the relation of reference or aboutness that a mental (and also linguistic) representation has to some target, whether concrete, abstract, or fictional. An image is an intentional structure in this philosophical sense because it represents or is about a scene, and the same is true of a belief that p because the belief is about p, where p is some fact; and likewise for other kinds of mental representations. Word and sentences inherit their intentionality, qua aboutness, from the mental representations, such as thoughts and beliefs, activated in their use.

The child's (and our) overall sense of minds is likely to *integrate* both notions of intentionality—purposefulness and aboutness—for general biological reasons and also more specific psychological reasons. This is an important point for the developmental story of reference and predication, which is why it deserves some elaboration. I begin with the biological reasons.

It is a biological fact that an organism cannot have intentional states in the philosophical sense of aboutness without being intentional in the ordinary sense of having or intending a goal. This is to say that an organism cannot have representations or some other ways of tracking the world without being goal directed or goal intended in the first place. And conversely, an organism cannot succeed in its goal-directed or goal-intended actions if it cannot represent or track its goals in the world (Bogdan 1994; Dretske 1989). It is therefore a matter of biological necessity that the intentionality of minds is intrinsically a *composite* intentionality (purposefulness and aboutness). I call this hybrid notion *purposed aboutness*.

I turn now to the psychological reasons. Since its job is to represent and predict how organisms relate to and act on the world, naive psychology would not be the adaptation it is without detecting and representing the purposed aboutness of conspecific minds. How it manages this job matters to the ontogenesis of reference and predication, and also begins to explain why nonhuman animals are not likely to refer and predicate.

There are *three basic components* in the naive-psychological representation of the purposed aboutness of another organism: a purposed *relatedness* to a target; the *direction* of this relatedness; and the *target* itself (Bogdan 2000, 2001). This parsing makes intuitive sense because these are indeed the components of our ordinary understanding of how organisms represent the targets of their actions. If I see a cat looking intently and intensely in some direction, I know that the cat is mentally related to some target out there. The cat's direction of gaze indicates the direction of its mental relatedness, and the bird in the distance looks like the (unfortunate) target. But I could miss the target and detect only the cat's mental relatedness (revealed by its behavioral posture and visual attention) and direction (revealed by its direction of gaze), or could notice just the mental relatedness. Our representations of words in conversation or reading also factor in the three dimensions in question: there are words intended to refer to—that is, relate to—nothing (e.g., bigbog, freshly invented); words intended to refer to something but misdirected (e.g., intellectual bacterium or square circle); and finally words intended to refer, successfully (most words, most of the time).

This tripartite parsing also makes psychological sense because it turns out that organisms may be able to represent some components of purposed aboutness but not others, with corresponding limitations in their sense of communicative reference. Thus, most species recognize the purposed world relatedness of other organisms as signs of life and agency, but only primates seem to recognize and follow the behavioral direction of that relatedness, as in gaze following, and humans alone represent the target of someone else's mental state or the target of a word or gesture (Povinelli 1996; Tomasello and Call 1997). These differences in which components of another organism's purposed aboutness are represented, and how, suggest different abilities at work. The representation of purposed relatedness or agency probably originates in a naive biology possessed by most species. Animals register the world relatedness of other animals in the eyes, bodily postures, movements, and other expressions of agency. The representation of the direction of an organism's purposed relatedness, apparently managed only by higher primates, may originate in a sophisticated yet only behavior-sensitive social cognition (Povinelli 1996) or a rudimentary naive psychology (Tomasello and Call 1997; Whiten 1991).

Representing Intent/ionality

No matter how nonhuman primates and possibly other species track the purposed relatedness of conspecifics and its direction, it seems to be done by representing only visible *behavioral* features, such as gaze, bodily posture, and movements. Such representations seem unable to determine objectively and reliably the target of that organism's intent, desire, attention, or interest. An observer of gaze or behavior, such as an ape or even a young child, determines the target of the action of a conspecific egocentrically and subjectively, in terms of the observer's own goals and what is immediately salient in the nearby environment. To determine objectively and reliably the target of an organism's desire or attention requires an ability to represent the *intended directedness* of those attitudes, and not just their behavioral expressions. This is what human naive psychology does, somehow. Without such an ability, an organism cannot understand symbol or word reference, and hence, according to the argument of the next chapter, cannot predicate either. The reason, as we shall see, is that it is the adult's intention to share attention with the child and direct her attention toward specific targets, including targets to be named by newly introduced words; and it is the child's task—intersubjective and naive psychological—to figure out the adult's intent (mostly from features of attention, voice, and behavior) and target directedness.

Infants and young children neither have intentions, as deliberate plans of action, nor recognize them in others. But they do have communicative *intents* and recognize such intents in others (Adamson 1995; Bretherton 1991). It was noted earlier in section 4.1 that as coregulative communicators, young children seem able to detect the mental subtext and the bilateral or child-oriented directedness of an adult's facial, emotional, and behavioral expressions. This amounts to saying that children register the adult's *intent as some sort of motive, initiative, and effort* to have such overt expressions affect the child, and be so recognized by the child—a pattern of communication that was codified earlier in a developmental reading of Grice's analysis.

At several key junctures in the early development of reference and predication, examined in the next chapter, the young child's recognition of bilateral communicative intent appears to join forces with and assemble the other two contributors to the child's sense of other minds—namely, the action-mirroring and naive-psychological abilities, both of which register mind-world relations. This assembly makes sense if we consider the existential challenges that the young child faces, and can meet only through interaction and communication with adults—coregulation, protection, reaching goals, learning a language, and assimilating the surrounding culture. These challenges presuppose figuring out not only the mental intent behind adult communications and actions but also their world directedness. Think, for example, of the adult showing the child how to play with a pet, handle a tool, or master a new behavioral routine by vocal instructions and actions to be watched and imitated. To figure out what the adult wants and teaches, the child must activate adult-interpreting abilities from all three clusters—register the mental intent of adult communication with mind-to-mind abilities, recognize and emulate the intent and pattern of adult actions with action-mirroring abilities, and represent the world directedness of regard, attention, bodily posture, and action with mind-to-world abilities—and as an important signal of feedback and reward, also convey a feeling of elation for success in the task or disappointment for failure.

As a result of this likely assembly process, when the child notices an adult looking at some target (and then at the child), the child represents not just the composite intentionality, qua purposed aboutness, of the adult's gaze but also, more specifically, its mental intent (e.g., to share the target with the child or call her attention to it). To coin a word for this mix of aboutness and intent, or intended aboutness, I will say that the child represents the *intent/ionality* of the adult's gaze, and similarly with the intent/ionality of other mental attitudes.

The child's early ability to represent the intent/ionality of the attitudes of others may result from a domain-specific set of ontogenetic adaptations to contexts of social interaction and communication. Although responding to specific and dated pressures of the first two or three years in the child's life, this set of adaptations is extremely potent in bringing about other crucial abilities, including referring and predicating. The implication here is not that normal adult ascriptions of attitudes always factor in a mental intent involved in communication. An adult can ascribe a belief or intention to a person without communicating or socially interacting with that person. The point is about *development* and specifically about how some ontogenetic adaptations install new mental faculties. As noted in the next chapter, without factoring in mental intent in representing world-directed attitudes—that is, without recognizing the intent/ionality of experiences and attitudes, particularly in shared attention—the child would not be able to acquire and assimilate words in mental schemes that will underpin predicative thinking.

Summation

Human communication initially develops along two independent tracks, for distinct and equally important biological reasons. One is a coregulative track that operates through bilateral exchanges of, and sensitivity to, the communicators' mental conditions that are bodily and behaviorally expressed, such as attention, emotions, and feelings, which reveal the intent to produce effects in the other mind—a harbinger of other-directed meaning. The other is an imperative track through which the young communicators aim to influence the behavior of others and also use others as social tools in reaching their goals. Neither track by itself is likely to turn into an explicitly declarative linguistic communication about the world. It looks like only a joining of forces can do the trick, since the child's coregulative communication is in the mental-sharing business and her imperative communication, particularly in its protodeclarative version, is in the business of communicating about the world. It is the child's sense of other minds that seems to be the first assembler of abilities originating in these disparate communication tracks, as it joins the representations of mental intent and aboutness in an enriched and composite naive-psychological category of intent/ionality.

The roots of the predication competence—coregulative communication, protodeclarative communication, and a sense of other minds—thus emerge for distinct developmental reasons and therefore have distinct primary functions, yet they contribute vital elements to the assembly of the predication competence. These elements can be graphically summarized in figure 4.1.

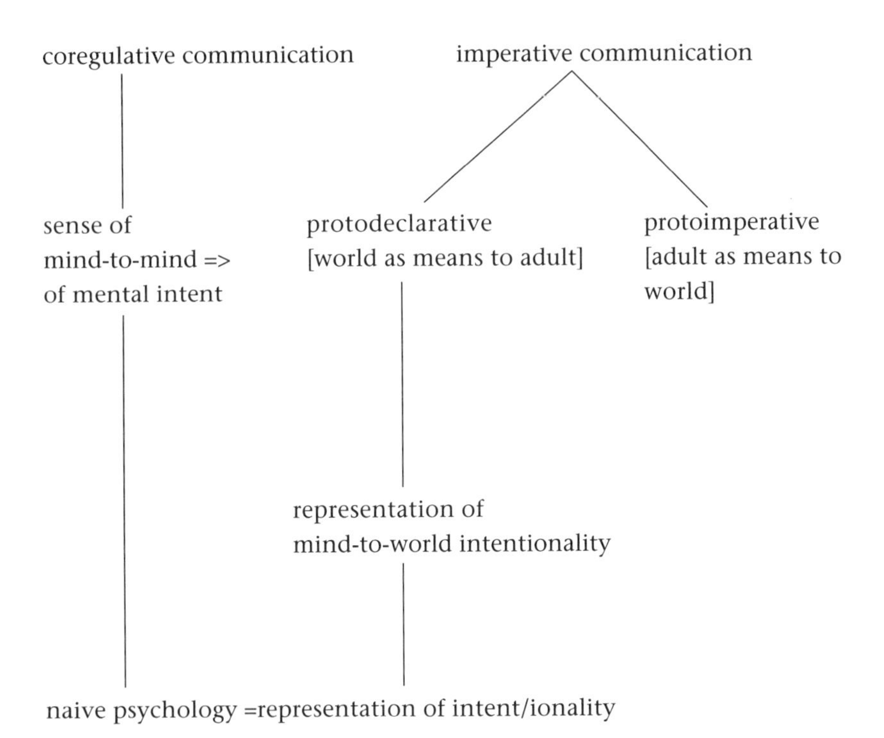

Figure 4.1
The roots of predication

The elements contributed so far by the three main roots of predication develop internally, in the child's mind, in response to challenges posed by physiological and then psychological coregulation and communication, and also by the world-bound and adult-assisted teleology of the child. As the next chapter contends, at several key steps on the ontogenetic staircase there will also be deliberate, active, and decisive external contributions by adults to the assembly of the predication competence.

5 Assembly

This chapter tells the story of the developmental assembly of the ability to predicate, in thinking and communicating, out of the ingredients surveyed in the last chapter. It is essentially the story of a series of increasingly more intricate joint child-adult ventures. It is in this sense that predication is a social construction. The basic idea is that these joint ventures enable the child to acquire words by exposure to the adults' explicit naming of targets of shared attention, which I will call *shared naming*. The child's mental schemes of shared naming and word usage based on it gradually reformat from inside her topic-comment communication in a predicative direction.

This process goes through several key stages. According to section 5.1, it takes an active adult participation to turn the earlier acquisitions of imperative protopredications, first, into the implicit form of joint child-adult-world triangulations and, later, into the more explicit form of shared triangulations. During this process, the child gradually forms a sense of the coreferential intent of the adult's mental states and actions, which is crucial to word acquisition by shared naming, as the next ontogenetic step to predication. Section 5.2 argues that the child's representation of shared naming becomes the mental template for ostensive or perceptually situated predication. According to section 5.3, this template in turn enables the child to master linguistic predication. Section 5.4 takes a look at the wider and later mental framework underpinning linguistic predication.

The argument of this chapter crisscrosses a vast territory of empirical data, many unknowns, and diverse theories competing to explain them. My journey will take drastic and opportunistic shortcuts, and stop only in the areas where I conjecture that the child's mental tools for predication are actively assembled.

5.1 Joint Ventures

Given what the child is able to do around her first anniversary, it appears that her coregulative and protodeclarative forms of communication with adults begin to join forces, and thus generate increasingly coordinated triangulations of objects and events in the world. My reading of the evidence is that these developments proceed according to a rather finely tuned choreography that integrates three contributions to predication: (a) the child's bilateral adaptations to adults; (b) the child's adult-assisted triangular adaptations to the surrounding physical and cultural world; and (c) the adult forms of intervention, scaffolding, and guidance, whose widespread and mostly spontaneous exercise seems to indicate evolved cultural practices of parenting and in general dealing with young children (Adamson 1995; Bates 1976; Bruner 1983; Hobson 1993; Rogoff 1990; Tomasello 1999).

This integration process seems to unfold in two stages. Their nature and timing are much debated in the developmental literature, but this need not concern us here (Adamson 1995; Eilan et al. 2005; Moore and Dunham 1995). I will extract, regroup, and relabel those least disputed elements that matter to the present analysis. To single out the elements that go into the development of predication and also avoid unwanted terminological associations, I call the first stage *joint triangulation* (mostly through joint gaze) and the second *shared triangulation* (mostly through shared attention). In both forms of triangulation, the child and the adult converge on a target visually as well as through communicational exchanges. What happens during these two stages gradually refines the coreferential relations between the topics and comments exchanged in child-adult communication, first implicitly and somewhat proximally, and later explicitly and distally, thus paving the way to word acquisition by shared naming and later linguistic predication.

Both forms of triangulation involve not only recognizing and tracking gaze and gesture but also a growing awareness of attention, whether directed at the partner or the triangulated target, or both. Whereas an awareness of gaze is an awareness of one looking in some direction, an awareness of attention indicates sensitivity to the mental focus, interest, intensity, and often intent of one's looking at or behaving toward some target. An awareness of someone else's attention, between the age of one and two, is one important effect, I think, of the incremental interplay of the child's early coregulative and bilateral intersubjectivity, on the one hand, and the world-bound and active protodeclarative communication, on the other hand. The child thus comes to understand someone else's attention as gaze or regard infused *with* mental intent and focus.

Joint Triangulations

The notion of joint triangulation is meant here to cover a variety of child-adult interactions with shared targets. These interactions develop mostly after the age of nine months. Michael Tomasello (1999, 62–70) distinguishes the following kinds of joint interactions: following one's gaze to a target, child-adult interactions mediated by a target, social referencing, pointing, and imitative learning of how to handle a new object. In social referencing, for example, the child takes an adult's emotional expression or behavioral response to guide the child's behavior toward something novel, surprising, or threatening. Pointing may also be construed as a protodeclarative invitation to share a target (Bates 1979, 103) or comment on a shared target (Baron-Cohen 1991, 240–243).

What these forms of joint triangulation seem to have in common is the *incompleteness* of the child-adult-world triangle: the child switches back and forth from looking at an external target and an adult, but has no sense, so far, of sharing the attention to a target with the adult. The adult-child side of the triangle is missing. On some accounts, the child may not even be aware of the adult's attention to a target (Baldwin and Moses 1994; Perner 1991). The evidence is far from conclusive, but it suggests that the bilateral intersubjectivity has not yet been fully integrated into the child's protodeclarative communication. This is why the child may not be able to discern the adult's coreferential intent, which is a later achievement of triangulation through shared attention.

In any event, the various forms of joint triangulation seem to me to highlight the work of distinct abilities that end up assembled or bundled into shared triangulation. Thus, social referencing manifests an intersubjective sense of the mental subtext and the child-bound directedness of an adult's communicative intent. The other forms of joint triangulation show the work of a naive psychology of gaze representation able to register and monitor an adult's visual (though not yet attention-driven) relations to the world. Some of these contributing abilities may be already integrated in the child's protodeclarative communication and imitative learning.

Some data provide a revealing glimpse into this gradual assembly process. David Leavens and Brenda Todd (2002) report that six-month-olds often alternate looking at a target of interest or excitement and a nearby adult, but do not distinguish between attentive and inattentive adults. This suggests that the child checks her interest in an external target with the adult's child-directed reaction—again, an incomplete, two-sided fragment of a potential triangle. What seems to be missing at six months is the protodeclarative communication intended by the child to capture and retain the adult's attention to a shared target. According to Bates (1976), protodeclarative communication develops at around nine months, which is when the child begins to engage in sustained joint triangulations of the sorts mentioned earlier.

It seems plausible to conclude that joint triangulations form a matrix in which protodeclarative communication emerges and operates. It is a matrix in which the child looks at, vocalizes, or gestures toward some external but nearby target of interest, and checks the adult's relation to the target and/or reaction to the child. The resulting communication has an external topic—proximal and rather vaguely defined—shared with an adult, is imperative, since the comments exchanged are sensitive to actions intended to reach a goal, and is egocentric, since the topics are represented only from the child's perspective and its terms. The child's priority is still to request adult attention and assistance. It makes sense at that age.

The main reason why the nine-month-old cannot yet recognize the socially triangulated target as the referent of someone's gaze, gesture, vocalization, or uttered word is the inability to represent an adult's *coreferential intent*. This is why, at this stage, adults often compensate for the child's failure to recognize coreferential intent by embedding their joint triangulations in helpfully scaffolded emotional and behavioral interactions (Adamson 1995; Bruner 1983; Rogoff 1990; Tomasello 1999). It is the context and/or the adults' helpful framing of the child's relation to a topic that largely manages their joint triangulations.

Ways of Naming

As we approach the stage of word acquisition, it is worth anticipating that there are at least three ways in which children may acquire words: learning by association (around six months), figuring out the namer's referential intent from various contextual, bodily, and behavioral clues (a few months later), and understanding coreferential intent through shared attention (twelve to eighteen months) (P. Bloom 2000, 61–65; Tomasello et al. 2005). I will argue that only the latter is conducive to predication, because coreference by shared attention alone has a communicational format that allows the child to register and then mentally schematize the connection between the topic-comment-presupposition format of the earlier child-adult exchanges, the adult's intent to direct the child's attention to a target to be named, and essentially, the child's use of the coreferential intent expressed by the word as a means to get the adult's attention in protodeclarative communication (note about First Words).

Shared Triangulations: A Sense of Coreferential Intent

Grasping an adult's coreferential intent in making a gesture or uttering a word or sentence is essential to the young child's understanding of what the adult is communicating about, in general. It is also essential for learning words by shared naming and embedding shared naming into a matrix of communication that involves a comment intently directed at a topic. This matrix in turn becomes the indispensable platform for predication. I construe *coreferential intent* as an adult's intent to refer to a shared target by making the intent manifest to the child, who recognizes and acknowledges it.

The main source of the child's understanding of coreferential intent is *shared attention*, which I distinguish from the standard notion of joint attention. There are disagreements, more serious than terminological, about how shared attention comes about and how it works [see note on Joint versus Shared Attention]. These disagreements are not important for our discussion, as long as we can identify those features of shared attention that are conducive to predication. There is good evidence that shared attention redesigns the child's naive psychology, communication, and word acquisition in the twelve- to eighteen-months interval. Dare Baldwin and Louis Moses (1994) suggest that "by the middle of the second year, infants understand that other people's attentional cues (line of regard, gestures) reflect their mental focus and referential intentions" (see also Adamson 1995; Bruner 1983; Tomasello 1999). From its timing and modus operandi, the ability for shared attention seems to assemble two previously separate lines of mental development:

1. The first line of development, based on the naive-psychological representation of another person's conative, emotional, and cognitive relations to the world, is the child's recognition that the adult is not just related to and aware of, because looking at, the same target as the child but actually *attends specifically* and *actively* to that target. The active mental directedness of the adult's regard—and not just the behaviorally determined direction of the gaze—seems to be explicitly recognized by the child in an objective and nonegocentric manner in a variety of contexts (Baldwin and Moses 1994). This seems to me to be one key component of the child's recognition of someone's intentful reference to a target in the world.

2. Connecting an earlier bilateral sense of shared mental intents with the new sense of an adult's active and specific attention to a target, the child becomes able to participate in the *shared and mutually acknowledged awareness* that each partner knows (a) that the other is intently and actively attending to the same target, and (b) that the other knows that they share this knowledge about their intended relatedness to the same target (Hobson 1993; Tomasello 1999).

The assembly of these two developments results in the child's *sense of an adult's coreferential intent.* On the comprehension side, the child recognizes that the adult intends the child to attend to the same target as the adult, and share this attention to the target; on the production side, the child intends the adult to do the same (Tomasello 1999, chapter 4). Shared attention makes such mutually intended coreference to a target possible. It enables the child to grasp someone's coreferential intent by joining the recognition of (bilaterally expressed) intent with that of (trilateral or world-bound) directedness—in short, by recognizing the *intent/ionality* of someone's attention (in the composite sense of the previous chapter, section 4.3). Differently worded, shared attention can be said to map the bilateral recognition of an adult's (child-directed) mental intent onto the directedness of the adult's mental states, in particular attention, manifested in its overt expressions. The result is the recognition of the coreferential intent of the adult's attention and later actions, utterances, and attitudes.

To put it more intuitively, imagine that the attention-sharing child notices an adult looking attentively at some target *X* and then looking intently at the child. The child represents not just the directedness of the adult's visual attention to *X* but also its child-addressed mental intent, which may be to share *X* with the child or call the child's attention to it. Each partner can be said to represent their shared-attention venture roughly as follows: "You intend me to attend to what you attend, and I do, because I recognize your intent, as you recognize mine as being similar to yours, and we share this mutual recognition." (For good graphic renditions of this reading, with naive-psychological and world-bound arrows going from each partner to the shared targets, and bilateral arrows going from one partner to another, see Tomasello 1999, 2003.)

I think that the child's mental advance toward coreference by shared attention works as well as it does because it mixes enough continuity with enough change to enable the child to assimilate novelty in manageable doses. The *change,* dramatic and full of consequences, is the assembly of the bilateral sense of intent and the naive-psychological representation of another person's intent/ional relations to the world. This novelty enables the child, for the first time, to perceive another person's attention as well as commenting expressions and reactions (earlier registered only bilaterally, as child addressed) as directed now at shared targets qua topics of mutual interest. The *continuity* consists in that for the child, shared attention may look like a new gadgetry for social interaction and communication, as were joint triangulations a few months earlier, and in the same protodeclarative and hence still imperative mode.

Since adults would insist on the new shared-attention format for joint triangulations and since the child still needs adults to reach her goals, the child is likely to assimilate the new adult-world-child coreferential triangulations by shared attention into mental schemes that still operate in the old imperative style as effective communication strategies directed at adults. The same will be true of the next step, which is acquiring a sense of word coreference—a momentous novelty, still embedded for a while in an imperative schematism of thinking and communicating. The child's assimilation of coreferential innovations—first through shared attention alone and then through shared naming—into prior protodeclarative schemes has the effect of incrementally smuggling in (as it were) and redesigning from inside what are already effective communication strategies to deal with adults.

5.2 Shared Naming

The next adult move in the arms race unfolding along the ontogenetic staircase is to exploit the new coreferential triangulations by shared attention to introduce children to words that are explicitly and intently directed at targets of mutual interest. These are words that children initially embed into their protodeclarative schemes of communication. The word reference relations introduced by this specific sort of naming have new properties whose eventual effect is to redesign the child's communication and thinking in a predicative format.

The Basic Idea

The ability to predicate originates in the young child's acquisition of words introduced intently and explicitly by adults in contexts of coreferential triangulation through shared attention. For brevity, I said that such words are introduced by *shared naming*.

Already noted, but in need of firm reemphasis, is the fact that not *all* words are learned through shared naming—certainly not the first words (around six months or so), and perhaps not most words afterward. Shared attention and shared naming are therefore neither necessary nor sufficient for word acquisition in general (P. Bloom 2000). But shared attention, with its form of coreferential triangulation, *is* necessary for word acquisition by shared naming and its role in the matrix of communication that involves a comment intently directed at a topic, and the latter in turn *is* necessary for the development of predication. This is because the word-acquisition scheme installed by shared naming in the child's mind becomes a template for predication when the scheme is used in, and as a result redesigns, the child's intentful and productive topic-comment-presupposition sort of communication.

Let me parse this basic idea in its key components. One component is that words learned through shared naming—and possibly only such words—fix in the child's mind the (Gricean-like) realization that (some) words refer because people explicitly and manifestly intend them to corefer in contexts of shared attention. This coreferential triangulation of shared targets is initially viewed by children as having the primary function of *intently directing the coreferential attention* of the partner to that target. Words acquired by means *other* than shared naming, and also many instances of pointing, may call one's attention to some target *without* an explicit intent to corefer to that target—that is, to share a mutually recognized and acknowledged relatedness to the target. Up to a point, young children may learn and employ words to call attention to some target imperatively but not coreferentially.

The notion that early words direct coreferential attention was proposed and elaborated by several developmental psychologists. Jerome Bruner's influential view was that word reference "is a form of social interaction having to do with the management of joint attention" (Bruner 1983, 68; shared attention in my terms). Nameera Akhtar and Tomasello (1998) write that "in comprehending a new word the child comes to understand that the adult is using the word to encourage her to focus her attention on one specific aspect of the current situation" (see also Tomasello 1999, 100–101). The analogy often drawn between pointing and naming goes in the same direction. In contexts of shared attention, the young child sees both pointing and naming as prompting and guiding coreferential attention. So construed, pointing is a gestural and sensorimotor form of naming intended to share reference with an audience (Bates 1979, 103).

Another critical component of the basic idea is that shared attention not only guides a partner's coreferential attention to a target but it also enables the partners to exchange *comments* about shared targets. Since in the prelinguistic contexts of shared attention, adults and children *already* communicate about the same targets by visually, affectively, and behaviorally commenting on them, the child would expect words introduced by shared naming to play an active role in the topic-comment-presupposition format of coreferential communication by shared attention. So it is fair to assume that in the child's eyes, the initial role of words acquired by shared naming is not only to direct coreferential attention to a shared target but also to elicit or make comments about it. This seems to be the case with many instances of pointing as well (Baron-Cohen 1991, 240–243).

Recall that the earliest comments, exchanged bilaterally and intersubjectively in coregulative communication, were analyzed (in chapter 4, section 4.1) as overt expressions of the intent to produce a mental effect in another person by making manifest some reaction, attitude, emotion, interest, or other state of mind. The overt expressions were looks, facial configurations, eye movements, gestures, vocalizations, and actions. In preverbal coreferential triangulations, these overt expressions do the *double duty* of directing attention to a shared target and expressing mental states as comments addressed to the interlocutor about the target. The proposal now is that in a first phase, the words acquired by shared naming begin to take over the *first* role of overt expressions, which is to *direct coreferential attention* to a target and activate the relevant concepts about it, leaving to looks, faces, voice intonations, and other *nonverbal* signals, the second (and already-known) role of expressing mental states as comments. As the child acquires more words by shared naming and weaves them into full utterances, and as the visual contexts of shared attention are increasingly replaced by the linguistic or virtual contexts of shared attention, predicate words and entire sentences begin to take over the *second* function of expressing comments on shared topics. This is how linguistic predication comes into existence. But the young child and my analysis are not yet there.

It is important at this juncture to bring in still another key component of the basic idea. There are good reasons to think that after the initial months of word acquisition by shared naming, children may develop a *virtual* coreference relation to adults, when they learn and employ words without adults around (Tomasello 1999, 117). Children also seem to assume adult coreferential intent for words whose referents are not perceptually present or clearly demarcated (Tomasello 2003). Even the child's solitary acts of pretense or self-addressed talk may also have virtual adults in mind (Harris 2000). Trevarthen (1993) has even suggested, rather controversially, that human infants are born with a dialogic mind and hence with a sense of the "virtual other."

In any event, it is widely accepted that the twelve- to eighteen-month-old's mental life is overwhelmingly tied to perception and action, and is largely imagistic (Bjorklund 2000; Perner 1991). As a result, what the child remembers, reenacts, or imagines—a particular situation, an experience, a communication context, or a learning pattern—is bound to be rerepresented in mostly imagistic or imago-motor terms. It should not then be surprising that the same may be true of the child's mental schemes of word coreference acquired by shared naming, since the latter is perceptually situated and imagistically represented by the child for quite a while. This analysis predicts that when the solitary young child uses a word to refer to a target, she may actually represent herself as directing the attention of a virtual coreferring adult to that target—at least in the early stages of word mastery. This may be part of the "internalization" of word acquisition—an influential idea first proposed by Lev Vygotsky (1962; see also Tomasello 1999, 125–129).

Although children begin to acquire words by shared naming around or soon after their first anniversary, it is only in the interval of eighteen to twenty-four months that they start to use *productively* language and such words in particular (Bates 1976; Tomasello 1999). Significantly, children begin to use words in self-talk and pretend play, hence again productively, around the same interval (Harris 2000; Olson 1989). As is the case in general with newly formed abilities, this fact suggests that eighteen-month-olds start to rehearse and hone their mental scheme for word reference, as a training ground for productive communication, even in the perceptual (but not imagistic) *absence* of the referent and the adult partner. All this matters because it is on the *production* side of communication that the child would best internalize, rehearse, and firm up the mental scheme for word reference, with a real adult in front of her eyes or a virtual one in her mind, and incorporate the scheme in communicative thoughts. One major impact of this incorporation is to turn communicative thoughts into predicative thoughts.

So much, then, for the basic idea. Before charting and empirically documenting the ontogenetic advance from word introduction by shared naming to predication, I note that at this critical turn in the developmental saga of predication, the map provided by the psychological literature gets somewhat vaguer and spottier, at least as far as I could determine. Whereas the study of language development and specifically word acquisition has been a booming industry for more than a century, and remains so, there are (to my knowledge) relatively few systematic analyses of the ontogenetic *debut* of predication (for notable exceptions, see Bates 1976; Olson 1989,

1993; more indirectly Hobson 1993; Tomasello 2003). The question that this book explores is not how, once launched, predication develops as part of language maturation. There is an ample psychological literature on this topic (Bates 1976, 1979; L. Bloom 1993; Nelson 1996; again Tomasello 1999, 2003; particularly Wall 1974). The question of this book is how predication *first* develops and why. It is a question about the origins of and reasons for the mental schemes responsible for predicative thoughts and utterances.

Ostensive Protopredications

Common observation and psychological data indicate that many words introduced by adults through shared naming take the form of (what may be called) explicitly *ostensive naming* addressed to the child and indicating some target *X* as

[this] is "X"

or

[that] is "Y,"

where [this] in (a) may be what the child and the adult jointly attend to perceptually, and [that] in (b) may be a target of pointing or head movement. The sounds of "X" and "Y" are all that the child registers. A more graphic rendition would be

[this] <— "X,"

where [this] is the target that the child perceives, and the arrow represents, in the child's mind, the adult's novel expressive device, in the form of the word "X," which intently directs the child's coreferential attention to the target.

Such acts of naming are *ostensive* or of a show-me sort. They make manifest or indicate their targets nonlinguistically through perception, shared attention, pointing, or some other action, often with the help of contextual and behavioral clues (Adamson 1995; Bates 1976; P. Bloom 2000). The adult usually follows the word introduction and the word's later use with some comment, as does the child. Their comments, directed at the word's referent, remain expressive in the already familiar and nonlinguistic form of looks, facial configurations, gestures, tone of voice, and the like. Seen in this light, the acquisition of words by shared naming probably looks to the child not as a novel and self-contained learning exercise but rather as part of a wider communicational envelope that is a continuation of a topic-comment-context form of shared attention by other means.

The result can be called *ostensive protopredication*: ostensive is the introduction and later use of the new word as a topic fixer, directing attention to the perceptually shared target like an indicator or a pointer; the notion of protopredication captures the fact that comments are made nonlinguistically about the target, mostly in an imperative or expressive mode. The child's productive use of ostensive protopredications follows the same format: the child uses a new word, with a topic-fixing role, to direct someone's attention to a shared target, about which the child produces some imperative comment, such as wanting *X*, or wanting to play with *X* or the like, through nonlinguistic means. So construed, ostensive protopredication is likely to be registered by the child as a new instance of continuity through change, and as such it best explains, I think, the child's

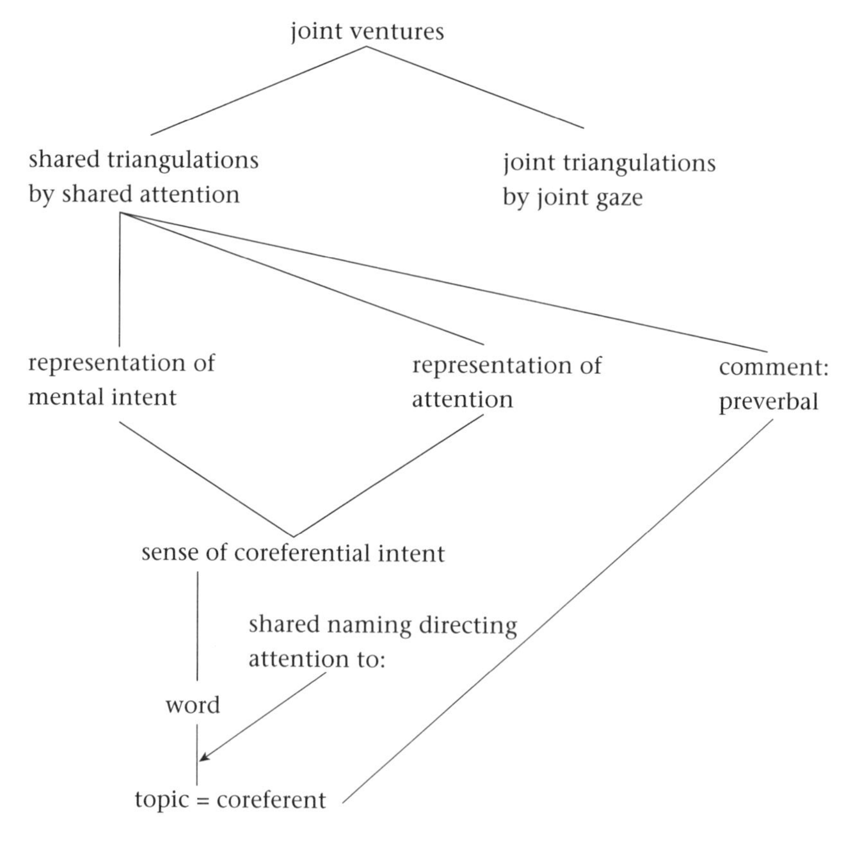

Figure 5.1
From joint ventures to ostensive protopredication

successful advance to predication on the ontogenetic staircase: one leg ahead while the other is still firmly placed behind on familiar ground. The process, so far, can be graphically summarized in figure 5.1.

Mental Scheme of Reference

In order to communicate effectively and successfully by means of words newly acquired by shared naming, the child faces the challenge of constructing a mental scheme for the reference relation between such words and their targets, particularly on the production side of her communication, and applying this scheme correctly in her communicative thoughts and utterances. The handling of this challenge has a crucial impact on the development of predication. What could that scheme be?

A plausible suggestion is that the sensorimotor image that the child uses to grasp word reference during the word-acquisition process, in the perceptual presence of the referent, is severed or decoupled from the actual perception of the referent, and comes to serve as the *meaning* of the word. When the child is in the presence of the actual referent and points at it, saying, "This [what is pointed at] is a cat," the child relates a sensorimotor scheme or percept currently representing the particular cat to a decoupled scheme or image stored in memory and representing (one may assume) a generic cat. Running this mental scheme is a split-level perceptual/symbolic mechanism (Bates 1976, 37, chapter 3; Olson 1989, 1993). The question is what this split-level scheme represents. Bates (1976) and Olson (1989, 1933) think that the use of this split-level scheme of word reference results in propositional predications. Bates also thinks that the predications are of the topic-comment format.

I think the split-level scheme of word reference contributes essentially, but does not yet amount, to predication. One reason is that not any sort of word acquisition and hence scheme of word reference will do. As noted already, early word acquisition, say from six to nine months, is likely to involve different mechanisms and result in different schemes of word reference—for example, associationist—and the referents themselves may be fuzzy and unparsed. Many and perhaps most other words are acquired without explicit naming addressed to children in contexts of shared attention, so again their reference schemes may be different (unless a virtual shared naming is reenacted by the child, at least in production). My view is that only the reference scheme of the words acquired explicitly by shared naming would contribute to the configuration of the predication competence. As far as I can tell, Bates and Olson do not distinguish among the various modalities of word acquisition, and hence among the resulting schemes of word reference.

Another and more central reason, detailed in the next section, is that by itself the application of a reference scheme of shared and explicitly ostensive naming does not yield a predication, and not even an ostensive protopredication. It takes comments to predicate or even protopredicate. In particular, it takes language-encoded comments that satisfy the intended descriptiveness and directedness conditions (on the list P) to generate predications. The twelve- to eighteen-month-old child is not yet there. To be effective and successful in the child's communication, especially on the production side, the reference scheme of words acquired by shared naming must develop further features that will be essential to linguistic predication.

Referential Altruism

To be successfully used in communication, the representation of the word reference relation must be *reciprocal*: what one partner understands a word to refer to is what the other does, and vice versa. How is the young child going to get this altruistic (or better: alter-centered) or nonegocentric stance on word reference? Since the young child is still an egocentric and imperative communicator, the answer to this question presages a dramatic change. For starters, let us note that modalities of word acquisition other than shared naming have a harder task of enabling speakers to view reference from the partner's perspective, nonegocentrically. Because of the underlying shared attention, with its reciprocity of coreferential intent, word acquisition by shared naming appears to have a built-in perspective switch, so to speak, at least according to Tomasello's account (1999, 2003).

Tomasello argues that the reciprocity of coreferential intent enables the child to engage in "role-reversal imitation," which consists in using a gesture or vocalization toward an adult in the same way that the adult uses it toward the child (an idea anticipated by Mead 1934, 109). Several facts noted earlier in this work, particularly in the previous chapter, as well as by Tomasello support this conjecture. One is that coregulative communication has already sensitized the child (since infancy) that adults have child-directed intents and child-directed mental states in general, and that these intents and states can be shared and mutually acknowledged. Shared attention builds on this sensitivity and turns it toward shared targets in the world. Another fact, at least according to one influential account, is that the child also has a sensorimotor and possibly affective "like-me" sense of another person (Gopnik and Meltzoff 1997). Even the action- and emotion-mirroring abilities (noted in chapter 4, section 4.3) may help here. Furthermore, the idea sketched earlier of the virtual other may enable the child to imagine and rehearse a communicative intent and its output in terms of how a possible audience would react. Finally, it may also help that from the child's perspective, most words appear to be so weird, unfamiliar, and arbitrary that only a cooperative and mutual fixation on their reference can secure their successful use.

All these considerations seem to lend credence to the claim that "the child can see herself from the outside, as it were . . . and comprehend the role of the adult from the same outside vantage point, and so, overall, it is as if she was viewing the whole scene from above, with herself as just one player in it" (Tomasello 1999, 99–100). Whether or not the child can or needs to imagine visually this shared frame of communication, it seems likely, for the reasons just surveyed, that her mental scheme of word reference operates under assumptions that reflect such a reciprocal view of word reference.

I also think that the child's reciprocal sense of word reference has a good deal to do with the precision of word coreference acquired by shared naming, as opposed to other forms of word acquisition. I will not develop this point here, except to observe, first, that this precision is related to a much sharper sense of being right or wrong when the naming is shared (on which more anon), and second, that autistic people, who are fairly egocentric in their cognition and communication, have a rather imprecise word semantics, at least as children (Hobson 1993). But as far as our discussion goes, the major contribution of referential altruism to predication consists in its role of securing the intended descriptiveness of the representation of the reference relation. This is my next topic.

Descriptiveness

Although most often formulated by an adult in a stipulative or even imperative manner, the word introduction by shared naming has the potential of bestowing declarative or descriptive force on the word reference relation. The shared-naming act tells the child that something, the name, relates to something else, the target named. Even though initially the child is likely to comprehend an adult's stipulation in imperative terms—for example, in terms approximating "let 'X' be the sound for [this]" or "I tell you [this] is accompanied by the sound 'X' "—in her thinking and productive communication the child will end up representing the word reference relation as something about which she can be right, but also often wrong, and that is therefore subject to correction.

In the other forms of word acquisition—learning by association, and figuring out the namer's world-directed referential intent from various clues—the link between a word and its referent is largely a hit-or-miss affair, and is reinforced or extinguished by the child's success or failure, respectively, to obtain what she wants by using the word. This is word acquisition by way of results, which is also typical of any tool use or behavioral routine. (It is what behaviorism usually thought about word acquisition. It works for animals and young children, but is not the distinctly human way, and not the one that leads to predication.) In contrast, the matrix of word acquisition by shared naming is shaped up gradually adding more constraints and structure at each major step on the ontogenetic staircase, and hence leaving less room for error about the identity of the target that is named.

As important is the child's likely realization that being right or wrong about the reference of words acquired by shared naming is not a matter of explicitly observing a physical event out there, or being successful or not in communicating with words, and thus getting what the child wants. What matters, in the new matrix, is the adult's reaction along with the resulting reciprocity and mutually acknowledged agreement in using a new word. More explicitly, for the child, referential success for words acquired by shared naming is a matter of reproducing and reciprocating the adult's coreferential intent, and acknowledging the adult's reactions to and corrections of the child's own communicative intent and output. At this stage of childhood, referential success is a social and indeed intersubjective matter of communication—an alignment of minds.

Essential to the success of the new matrix of word acquisition is the fact that the word-introducing ostension by shared naming is *explicitly represented* by the child (although it is still partly linguistic and partly perceptual): its components (word and referent) and the intent/ional relation between them are made visually as well as vocally or gesturally manifest by the adult through shared attention, and are distinctly recognized as such by the child. The child encodes each component and the connecting reference relation through distinct representations generated by distinct abilities: the target of coreference through shared perceptual triangulation; the vocal or gestural word by appropriate perception, and a dedicated sensitivity to adult forms of sharing attention to topics of mutual interest; and the intent/ional relation of word reference through the (earlier) bilateral representation of the adult's intent (now) embedded in target-directed shared attention.

There is, then, an explicitly relational truth or falsity about the representation of the reference relation of a word acquired by shared naming, particularly when it is initially regarded by the child as two intent/ional arrows—one directed at the child, and the other at the target, thereby making manifest to the child that the word, and the commenting looks, gestures, and vocalizations, are about that target as a shared topic and thus coreferent (roughly, Tomasello's picture). It is the child's representation of these intent/ional arrows triangulating the two partners and the coreferent that distinguishes word acquisition by shared naming from naming by association, where a new word may at best be represented as merely coinstantiated with its referent, and also from figuring out from sundry clues the adult's simple, unshared referential intent, where (again) a new word may be represented as coinstantiated with the referent of the intent.

The explicit representation of shared word reference, construed by the child in trilateral intent/ional terms, and constantly confronted with the adult reactions and corrections, tell the child that naming relations have truth conditions of a special sort. When an adult questions the child's grasp or use of a name, particularly in front of its referent, the child cannot fail to see that the question is intended to be factual, pointing to an actual intent/ional relation about which one can be right or wrong. Andrew Lock (1980, 121) suggests that the adult questioning of the child's mastery of a name may actually scaffold the development of the propositional format of speech. I think the scaffolding is done by the shared naming itself, but the questioning is bound to reinforce in the child's mind the facticity and truth evaluability, and hence the intended descriptiveness of the shared-naming relation and also its implicit social normativity, as noted next.

Social Obligations

Shared naming—and it alone, I think—introduces the child to words as *conventional symbols*. Words *are* conventional symbols anyway, but only shared naming enables the child to *represent* them as such. Since I do not want to complicate the analysis with explicating such complex and much-debated notions as convention and symbol, I will limit myself to extracting only those aspects that have a *developmental* (as opposed to general) significance consistent with the present discussion. I would suggest that for the child, communication becomes *symbolic* when specific gestures, vocalizations, and finally words are understood as having the visible intent—later regimented as a permanent and invisible function—of *initially* coreferring to specific and shared targets, even though, and precisely because, there is nothing visibly in common between the relata on the two sides of the coreference relation. And for the child again, communication becomes *conventional* when there is mutual coordination and acknowledgment between the child and the adult about specific words-as-symbols being intended to have specific coreferents treated in the same way by both partners (Hobson 2003; Tomasello 1999, 2003).

This analysis places most of the initial burden of what counts for the child as conventional symbol on the child's recognition and mutual acknowledgment of coreferential intent. Natural signs, signals, or words merely associated with the things and events they communicate about, *without* a recognized and mutually acknowledged coreferential intent, are unlikely to be treated by the child as conventional symbols. Lacking shared attention as a platform for the recognition and acknowledgment of coreferential intent, neither animal nor infant communication is apt to become conventionally symbolic. The same is true of early words acquired through association or clever guessing, or by registering an adult's referential intent from various clues or through adult scaffolding. Even though the words so acquired are conventional symbols, the child is unlikely to treat them in this light, prior to shared naming.

In short, conventionally symbolic communication works only if both parties, and the child in particular, recognize the intended descriptive correctness of the reference to a target and its implicit social normativity, in the sense of being obligatorily the same for everybody engaging in such communication. Again, this recognition need not take the form of explicit representations in the child's mind (except, perhaps, in cases of violations or challenges). It suffices that the child's mental scheme of word reference assumes or factors in such recognition, in the sense that the scheme would not work well or at all without it.

The Commenting Part

If the analysis so far is on the right track, then what is remarkable about the child's mental scheme of word coreference acquired by shared naming, as a component of ostensive protopredication, is that it begins in an imperative mode, but ends up acquiring an intended descriptive form because of its intent/ional truth conditions and normative force, and because of the symbolically conventional character of the word coreference relation. This unusual metamorphosis makes such a mental scheme of word coreference a vital fulcrum that turns the child's communication and thoughts from imperative into declarative and predicative, respectively.

The metamorphosis begins with words that direct attention to a shared target as topic—potential subjects in a normal predication. The next question is how this metamorphosis extends to the remainder of the child's ostensive protopredications.

So far in my story, the child's ostensive protopredication has remained imperative in both calling attention to a shared target as topic and making or eliciting comments directed at it. Suppose, for example, that the adult says the word "cat" in front of a cat, and makes a gesture or adopts a facial expression, as comment, which the child recognizes as (say) "sleepy," "hungry," or whatever. As I read the evidence (Adamson 1995; Bruner 1983; Hobson 1993; Rogoff 1990; Moore and Dunham 1995; Tomasello 1999), the content of what the adult's gesture or face conveys is most probably treated by the child as a *two-pronged* comment that is (a) *addressed to the child* and intending the child to see it (b) as *directed at the referent* of the word "cat." This two-pronged format of the comment is familiar to the child from prelinguistic triangulations by shared attention. It is therefore reasonable to infer that the linguistic novelty for the child at this protopredicative stage is that *words* mediate and guide the coreferential attention to targets as shared topics, and invite comments about those topics. This half-linguistic protopredication remains intrinsically social, even when practiced in solitude with a virtual other in mind—a way of managing shared attention by means other than directly visual. Again, there is continuity through change. But there are further and more radical changes along the way, or rather up the ontogenetic staircase to predication.

5.3 Linguistic Takeover

Linguistic predication assembles and organizes words into sententially expressed propositions. How does this come about? How does the child's mind transit from ostensive and half-linguistic protopredication to full linguistic predication? The following answer is among the most attractive.

Quine's Gambit

Its basic idea is that words acquired ostensively, perhaps on the model of the previous section, can be combined by the child to handle word-to-word predications. Suppose the words in question, already mastered by the child, are "lawn" and "green." In the presence of a green lawn, the child also learns to associate "lawn" and "green" into "green lawn" or even "the lawn is green." The child knows perceptually that the lawn is green and may even assent to the adult question "green lawn?" but so far her linguistic mind grasps only an association of words in the presence of a green lawn. This is coinstantiation through multiple acts of naming. The child can also think of a lawn and, separately, a green expanse, even when not perceiving them, courtesy of her memories and mental images. So now, on hearing the word "lawn," the child can think of the word "green" and what it represents. The association of the words is now linguistic and their combined meaning is (let us suppose) mentally imagistic. The meaning of "lawn" (image under concept) is now linked to the meaning of "green" (also image under concept). The ostensive phase, when the child associated the word "green" with a currently visible lawn, is now replaced by a fully linguistic phase, when the word "green" is associated with the word "lawn"—a transfer from what is seen to what is said. Is the result linguistic predication?

The reader may have recognized here a reading of Quine's account (1974, 63–67) of the ontogenesis of predication and its connection with word acquisition. It is a simplified reading, but I think adequate for our discussion. Quine thinks that the answer to the last question (is it predication?) is yes, and that the transfer in question does result in full and genuine linguistic predication—the predication of the standing or eternal sentence, as he puts it. The mechanism that transforms word ostension into predication, according to Quine, is that of a "transfer of conditioning" (65).

I see problems and ironies in Quine's account. One problem is that Quine's actual explanation of word acquisition is not ostensive protopredication, in the sense developed in the previous section, but straightforward association of the behaviorist sort. About the first words, Quine is rather optimistic: "Infant learning is a bright domain, and there behavioristic psychology blooms. The beginnings of language are learned ostensively. The needed stimuli are right out there in front, and mystery is at a minimum" (35). This, as noted, may be true of the period between six and nine months. As for later, one wishes it were so simple. Developmental psycholinguistics no longer buys this behaviorism of word-referent association, for good reasons, some amply discussed earlier in this chapter.

Another problem is that if Quine were right about word acquisition by associative ostension, then his account of predication, through the transfer of conditioning, ought to deliver *only* a coinstantiation of word meanings rather than predication. Far from magically converting stimuli-words associations into word-to-word predications, the transfer of conditioning merely joins words in some predictable associations, in the absence of perceptual stimuli. The result ought to be what Quine himself calls an attributive compound, or what I called a coinstantiation, whose composite meaning somehow joins two distinct mental images under appropriate concepts.

The irony here is that Quine convincingly distinguishes between observational compounds, assembled through thematic coinstantiation, on the one hand, and predications, on the other hand. The child learned "lawn" and "green" separately, and on now hearing these words together, joins and superimposes their mental images. The result is still an observation or occasion sentence. Although "green lawn" is a thematic coinstantiation, whereas "the lawn is green" has the grammatical form of a predication, this, for Quine, seems to be a distinction without a difference. And so it is. The copula "is" is of the coinstantiation sort.

I would not be surprised if some symbol-learning animals could form such name-combining coinstantiations. The latter have all the makings of a joining of elements in a predication *minus* its unity. If they have some sort of unity, as already noted, it is likely to be behavioral or instrumental, having to do with the animal's behavioral routines and goals. This is not the unity of predication. The main reasons are the lack of intended directedness from one of its elements to another and the underlying topic-comment-presupposition format that would frame this directedness into a predicate-to-subject structure. The intended directedness is usually (though not always) reflected in the copula "is." The "is" of predication remains a mystery in Quine's account, as it does, psychologically speaking, in most accounts of predication.

The same diagnosis works against Quine's account of the predicativeness of standing or eternal sentences. Even in the absence of perceptual stimuli, there is nothing in his account to prevent the child's assent to or use of the sentence "the lawn is green" from being the mere coinstantiative construction whose composite meaning joins two distinct images under concepts. This is a reading encouraged by Quine's associationist view of word learning in general. The explanation of linguistic predication is still elusive.

Before turning to the explanation I propose, I note that Quine's account might also be recruited to explain how early humans may have had—just like young modern children have—a rich enough vocabulary and even a versatile communication gadgetry without necessarily having a predication competence. Linguistic coinstantiation is likely to precede linguistic predication. I return to this idea in the next chapter.

Linguistic Coinstantiation

Continuity through change would suggest that the young child's early mastery of the predicative copula (or its mental equivalent) follows the early pattern of, and may be mentally modeled on, her previous understanding of word acquisition by shared naming. That earlier understanding is often checked when the reference relation is queried or challenged by an adult, as in "is [this] an 'X'?" or "what is [this] called?"—where [this] is a perceptually shared referent of the word in question. In such cases, the child may see the copula as directing attention to the word's referential relation to a visually shared target, or as reidentifying the word's reference relative to a stored schema or image (i.e., meaning) associated with the word.

Likewise, we may conjecture, the *early* uses of the copula (or its mental equivalent) with predicate words may be construed by the child as signaling the intent to direct instances of their meanings, encoded as stored schemata or images, at the referents of subject words. For example, when the child predicates—or hears the predication—that "this cat is white" and knows what "white" means, she may think, in this particular case, of the meaning of "white" as intended to refer to the animal in front of her, the cat, just as "cat" is intended to refer to the same animal. One difference from the earlier ostensive protopredication "[this] is cat" (where [this] was a perceptual given) is that now, in a full linguistic expression, the referent in the subject position is picked out by a word, the word "cat," not by perception alone. Another and crucial difference is that the child now knows, after a variety of naming experiences and reinforcements, that "cat" refers to an objectlike sortal and "white" to a property-like sortal. Children, like many animal species (recall Bermudez's account from chapter 2, section 2.3), have a naive physics that enables them to recognize separately objects, properties, and relations. In acquiring words, children place labels or symbols that track these distinct sortal categories.

In a first stage, to master linguistic expressions like "this cat is white," the child must compute the fact that "white" applies to what "cat" does, hence that "white" is another name whose primary function is (again) to direct attention to a target (cat) and invite a comment—which is still preverbal. This is why the whole computation is still prepredicative. On this analysis, then, one should not be surprised to find (perhaps experimentally) that the child's first full linguistic formulations, such as "cat is white," may be actually represented by the child's mind as sequential acts of alternative or multiple coreference through shared attention with a real or virtual partner. The child was said to know already, perceptually, naive physically and prior to language, that cat and white may be thematically related (as object-property), but the *entry* of this knowledge in (and its alignment to) the newly developing language may be mediated by the child's early representation of "cat is white" and other thematic combinations of linguistic expressions (agent-action, object-relation-object, etc.) as sequences of such acts of alternative or multiple coreference.

Is the resulting linguistic expression "cat is white," and others like it, predication? Not yet, I think. For one thing, the comment is still outside the scope of the linguistic expression and still managed in the good, old, preverbal way, by means of looks, gestures, faces, giggles, and so on. The child still construes "white" as a coreferring name for an aspect of the cat, not as a comment about the cat. From the fact that the child knows that "cat" refers to the animal as object and "white" to one of the animal's property, it does *not* follow that the child construes the word "white" (or its meaning, rather) as a predicate. All that follows is that the child has managed to express a coinstantiation of cathood and whiteness linguistically—something that Bermudez's animals managed to do only mentally, according to the earlier argument of chapter 2, section 2.3.

This is to say that the topic-comment format and the predicate-to-subject directedness have not been yet fully blended and absorbed into language use. Furthermore, by understanding that "white" applies to the same referent as "cat" (and likewise for other combinations), the child has only brought thematic coinstantiations fully within the scope of language. The copula (or its mental equivalent) so far has the prepredicative function of directing attention to the fact that a word applies to what another word applies, thus tokening a thematic coinstantiation. This is why, I speculate, one (whether an early human, a modern child, or a modern adult even) can have a fully developed language along the dimensions on the list S, and only coinstantiate and even flexibly combine various coinstantiations, but not predicate. No matter how routinized and hence unconscious the practice of predication will become, its initial mastery requires a *further* mental act of intending to direct the meaning of a predicate, *as a comment*, to the referent of a subject, and to have this intent recognized, all of this within a topic-comment-presupposition matrix of thinking and communicating. On the ontogenetic staircase to predication that she is still climbing, the young child is not yet there.

Linguistic Comment

The copula (or its mental equivalent) acquires full predicative force when the linguistic utterance is recruited to work as a topic-comment structure, and therefore when the comment itself becomes fully linguistic. An interesting clue to the transition from the ostensive and half-linguistic protopredications to coinstantiative linguistic expressions, and finally to linguistic predications—a transition likely to be gradual (Bates 1976), combining again continuity with change—is that the child's early linguistic predications remain perceptually situated for quite a while, as probably does the child's grasp of word reference in general. The informed opinion is that until about three to four years of age, most of the child's linguistic predications remain tied to communicational interactions with others in contexts of shared attention, and thus are construed by the child as linguistic comments on topics that are visually present or virtually present in memory (Bates 1976; Tomasello 1999).

In time, even if the context and the presuppositions remain perceptually situated, the subject words no longer function solely as perceptual topic fixers, by directing the partner's visual attention to shared targets, and begin to operate more generally. Nevertheless, for the child, the context remains one of actual or virtual attention shared with an adult, but the shared attention is increasingly *linguistic* rather than perceptual. The child becomes able to use what is *said* to fix a linguistically shared topic that is open to linguistically predicative comments (Bates 1976, 97).

The names for properties, relations, and other more complex combinations that, as suggested earlier, first operated inside linguistic coinstantiations, take over as linguistic predicates intended as comments that add new information or express an attitude to topics and presuppositions already shared. During this still-formative period, the child is likely to intend such linguistically formulated comments to produce mental effects in an (actual or virtual) audience by calling attention to the predicative comments being directed at a topic.

The suggestion, then, is that the child's *initial* (repeat: initial) understanding of linguistic predication is tied to a communication context, and consists in *representing a predicate word as a comment addressed to a present or virtual audience, and calling the audience's attention to the meaning of the predicate word being intently directed at the referent of the subject word.* Intuitively, when the child says, "Mommy, look, the cat is asleep" (which the cat is most of the time, anyway), the child's initial use (and grasp) of her predication is likely to consist in intending the predicate word ("asleep") to alert the mother that its meaning (being asleep) is directed by the child as a comment on the visually shared, but now named, topic, the cat in question, and have the mother acknowledge this intent. This is the linguistic successor of the two-pronged commenting strategy (i.e., addressing the interlocutor and directing her attention to the subject as a topic) used in ostensive protopredications.

The story, so far, of linguistic predication and the role of the copula can be graphically summarized in figure 5.2.

I have not found direct empirical evidence for this line of analysis, although I detect elements of it in the analyses of Bates (1976) and Olson (1989, 1993), and general compatibility with the psychosocial analyses of word acquisition of Bruner (1983), Hobson (1993), and Tomasello (1999, 2003). These latter analyses emphasize the tight connection between shared attention and the mastery of word reference. This is the basis for the hypothesis that the child's early understanding of word coreference by shared naming is likely to be a template for grasping predication. Without the representation of word coreference as intently directing one's attention

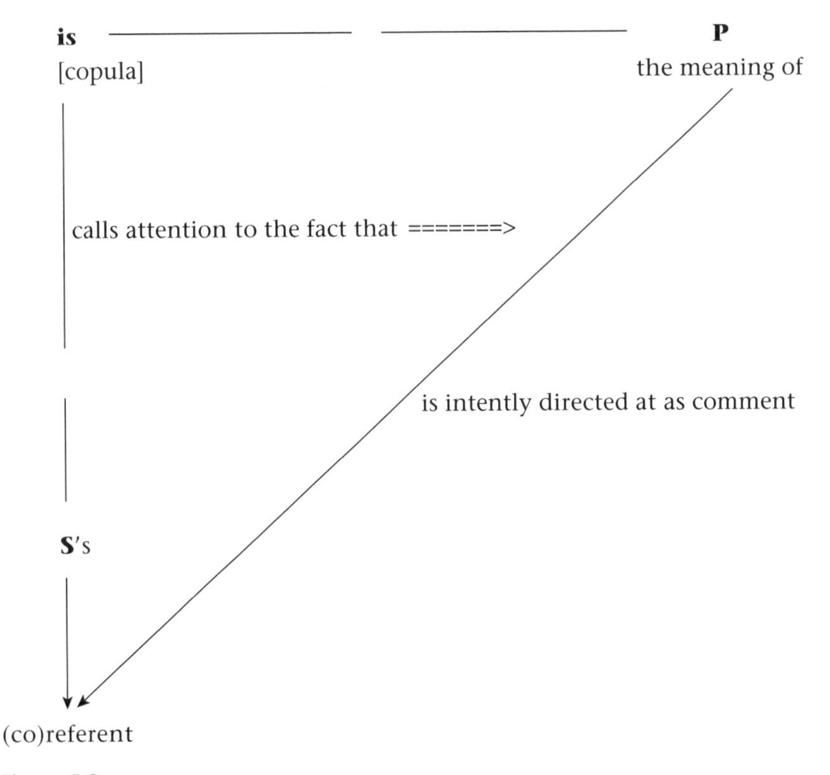

Figure 5.2
The child's initial grasp of the linguistic predication [S is P] and of the copula "is"

to a shared target, the topic-comment-presupposition communication would not turn predicative. The representation of word coreference is the fulcrum that does the turning. There is, therefore, no predication without words—not in the sense of words expressing or encoding meanings, as usually assumed, but first and foremost in the sense of the mental redesign effected by the very acquisition of words (specifically through shared naming).

Predicative Descriptiveness

The earlier conjecture that predications are preceded by linguistic coinstantiations, in the form of sequential acts of multiple coreference, could explain how the child's earliest predications become *descriptive* (and hence, truth conditional) in terms of the early mental scheme of word acquisition. The conjecture could explain in particular why the intended directedness of the meanings of predicate words to the referents of subject words, usually handled by the copula (or its mental counterpart), is represented by the child as *obligatorily* descriptive, as was the case earlier with the child's representation of the reference of ostensively acquired words.

Consider, again, the simple predication "the cat is white." The child's initial acquisition of "cat" and "white" had the function of an attention director, and was successfully carried out only if represented as a descriptive, truth-sensitive relation between a word and its referent—a relation about which one can be right or wrong. Now the conjecture is that in its commenting role, "white" is intended to refer to the referent of "cat" with the same likely representation. Addressed to an interlocutor, the use of "white" as a comment is intended to call attention to the fact that its meaning is directed at the referent of "cat." This function of attention director succeeds only if, again, "white" manages to refer to an aspect of what "cat" refers to—a relation that is also descriptive and truth conditional. Recall that the function of attention director is imperative, yet its success depends on the child's representation of a descriptive reference relation (continuity through change). The result is that a predication begins to be understood by the child as truth conditional and thus truth-valuable in a specifically topic-comment-presupposition format.

Since comments are intently directed at topics in contexts of shared attention, the child comes to understand the shared-naming relation and later predication as intended to be descriptive. The intended descriptiveness of predication is thus quite different from the implicit and passive descriptiveness of coinstantiative representations of the formal and psychological sorts discussed in chapter 2, and quite different from the similarly implicit and passive descriptiveness of visual or memory images that are subject to recognition patterns and categories.

One can say, somewhat metaphorically, that predication puts the passive coinstantiative mind of the young child in a conscious and voluntary intent/ional motion, thanks to the initial stimulus and framework provided by shared naming. As a coordinated mental activity, shared naming forces the young child to realize that representations (verbal, symbolic and finally mental) can be intently directed at various targets (visibly shared, initially, and later more abstract), that the intended directedness succeeds only if acknowledged by an interlocutor, and that this interpersonal acknowledgment in turn succeeds only if the intended directedness of shared naming is descriptive and socially normative. Building on shared naming, predication absorbs all these intent/ional novelties into the very fabric of the child's propositional thinking.

The Unity Problem Revisited

It is fitting to conclude the story of the developmental assembly of the competence for predication by reflecting on what it tells us about the unity of predicative thoughts (i.e., the fact that they are more than the sum of their parts). As mental representations that feed into thinking and guide action or communication, thoughts normally are unitary. Their unity resides in what makes them mentally and behaviorally functional, and hence causally efficacious. This is true of coinstantiative as well as predicative thoughts. The general question, then, is how to explain the functional unity of thoughts, both coinstantiative and predicative. And the more specific question, central to this book, concerns the functional unity of predication.

As for the general question, it may help to think of the unity of thoughts as a version of the more general *binding* problem of cognition—actually, *two* binding problems, I think. One, concerning the *binding of representations*, is the problem of constructing coherent and stable representations of objects, properties, and other items out of fragmentary, partial, and transient input stimuli from various modalities, such as vision, hearing, or touch. The human visual processing, for example, begins with retinal excitations that pick up proximal light patterns, and ends up with coherent images of trees and houses along with their size, color, and other properties. The binding problem here is how the visual system manages to bring together and integrate, in successive computational steps, disparate encodings of various pieces of visual information into a final representation of a recognizable object, such as a tree or a house. The evolved solutions, for various species, are likely to reflect pressures and constraints on what an organism must frequently recognize and judge in order to act on.

The other binding problem, which depends on the solution to the first, concerns the *binding of judgments*. This is the problem of how to bind representations of objects, properties, agents, actions, and other thematic items into composite, categorically or conceptually structured judgments that cause and guide further cognitions as well as appropriate actions. Animal species and (most likely) human infants evolved the *coinstantiation* solution to the judgment version of the binding problem: thematic representations (as solutions to the first binding problem) are somehow joined or sequenced in ways that provide adequate recognition of structured facts and events in the environment that afford opportunities for action or communication. Such coinstantiative judgments possess unity, their own kind of coinstantiative unity, if, when, and as long as they do their normal work in the organism's communication and action, according to the appropriate evolutionary script. This "if, when, and as long as" is a qualifier intended to avoid the temptation—often present in the psychological literature (see chapter 2)—to see predication in animal or infant minds just because they are found experimentally or observationally to have the right thematic representations of objects, properties, actions, and so on, as solutions to the first binding problem. It should take additional and independent research to establish how these thematic representations are woven into what kind of judgments. My educated guess has been that animal and infant judgments have coinstantiative, but not predicative, unity.

The *predicative* unity of human judgments is due to distinct yet gradually converging developments, most of them uniquely human, as far as I can tell. These developments end up reorganizing the young child's coinstantiative judgments along new dimensions—the P-dimensions. In particular, a predicative judgment owes its unity to the exercise of two P-abilities—to direct intently and explicitly the meaning of predicate words at the referents of subject words, in the form of comments about topics, relative to some presuppositions; and to signal or express the intent to do so (which at least in the formative stages of early childhood, also involves having this intent acknowledged by an interlocutor in communication). On the production side, it is the very act of predication, exercising these P-abilities, that confers unity on its output; on the comprehension side, the unity results either from the direct recognition of the predicative act, as in direct communication, or from its inferential recognition, as in reading or indirect speech. It takes a P-able mind actively to unite thematic representations into a predication, and it takes another P-able mind actively to project inferentially unity into an utterance that is heard or a sentence that is read.

The implication, then, is that there is no predication without predicating. Just as, relatedly and more basically, there is no topic-comment-presupposition structure without the act of commenting on a topic, and as relatedly and still more basically, there is no meaning without the act of meaning something (in Grice's sense) in communicating and thinking. The child's progression from bilaterally meaning (the act) to commenting on topics to intently coreferring to predicating revolves around a gradual buildup of successive kinds of mental *acts*—a fundamental fact of development, which should not be obscured by the later routinization and fossilization of the outputs of these acts in thinking and language use. The P-abilities that generate the unity of predication continue to be operative in adult communication and thinking, especially when the thinking is done by talking to oneself. Even when, later, the audience drops out of the child's mental picture, linguistic predication is likely to continue to work in the child's (and adult's) mind according to the same functional model.

Kant was right, after all: the human mind is a synthesizer and unifier of a special sort, which is not the association sort, as Hume and the empiricists believed, and as argued here, is not the coinstantiative sort either, as many other philosophers and psychologists believe. As Kant maintained, human thinking recruits, activates, and integrates the outputs of several mental faculties, such as perception, memory, recognition, conceptualization, reasoning, and more. But even this Kantian-style synthesis, although necessary for predication, and so salutary in emphasizing the mental activity involved, is not yet sufficient for predication. It takes the specific and rather unusual P-abilities to reach that sufficiency. These are abilities that can be discerned and understood mostly—if not only—in developmental terms, because they are constructed psychosocially during development, mostly for reasons specific to distinct stages of development.

Transition

The crucial and much-neglected P-dimensions of predication have thus been accounted for, developmentally. Officially, the argument of this book is over. Linguistic predication was shown to emerge at the top level of the ontogenetic staircase previewed in chapter 3. This was the advertised agenda of this book. The reader wary of, or not interested in, further developments as well as some implications and speculations may usefully stop at this point, without missing the essentials. I, for one, would go a few steps further, in the next section and the chapter that follows. One such step, taken below, suggests that as further and strong support for the developmental story told so far, there is fairly good evidence that linguistic predication continues to work in the matrix of comments that are intently directed at topics relative to presuppositions. It is a matrix that prelinguistically preceded predication, made it possible, and continues to run it as part of normal thinking and language use.

5.4 Thinking Predicatively

The guiding metaphor for what follows is that of an iceberg. The tip of the iceberg is a predicative thought, normally condensed and expressed in—or sometimes even mentally imaged as—a sentence or utterance in some natural language. Let us call this the *surface expression*, and let us call the underlying matrix of comments that are intently directed at topics relative to presuppositions the *deep predication*. Without the rest of the iceberg, and hence the deep predication, factored into the explanatory equation, it is easy to yield to the tempting idea that the predicativeness of a thought can be fully accounted for in terms of its surface expression, which explicitly exemplifies the S-dimensions, and thus its minimal and coinstantiative propositional content. This is the temptation I criticized in chapters 1 and 2, particularly as it influenced the psychological analyses of predication.

Said versus Meant

When the iceberg below the tip is brought into the predication equation, the propositional content of the thought at the tip changes from what looks on the surface as minimal and coinstantiative to predicative. Consider, as an instructive analogy, the familiar distinction between what is said, in the sense of verbally represented, and what is meant. Suppose we are at an academic party, and I say to you, "It is getting late." You understand the literal meaning of what I say (that it—the time of the day—is late), but you also understand the *intended* meaning that (for example) it is time to leave, or I am tired or bored (bored is more like it). Your grasp of the intended meaning factors in aspects that need not be part, nor literal entailments, of what I literally said. These are aspects such as my tone of voice, facial expression, recent reactions of what was happening around us, memories of similar past situations, and so on. Such collateral aspects, which we both assume we share, make our communication intelligible and successful. Dan Sperber and Deirdre Wilson (1986) have analyzed in great detail and with a wealth of illustrations the distinction between literal and intended meaning, and the notion of shared assumptions (see also Clark and Clark 1977).

Taken in isolation from a context and a communicative intention, the literal meaning of what I said (that it is getting late)—and in general the literal meaning of what is said—is bound to be minimally propositional and hence not predicative. If this sounds counterintuitive, it is because our (deep) predicative minds almost never treat a literal meaning in such isolation. We cannot help but read predicativeness in a literally expressed thought. The exception may be a warning seen on a computer screen or a traffic poster, but even then we may be prone, spontaneously, to read an intended and therefore a predicative meaning behind it. (Homework: Think of a parrot who sees me or anybody yawning, and as trained says, "It is getting late." Is the parrot predicating? Is the parrot meaning anything intendingly? That is, does the parrot mean or intend to communicate, about, say, the time of the day [topic], that it is late [comment]?)

But the isolation from context and communicative intention may be operative when adopting the folk-psychological mode of reporting or describing thoughts, and when, as a result, it becomes easy and tempting to identify predication with coinstantiation (and meaning with just semantic content). This is because as folk psychologists, we ordinarily report or describe thoughts, of others and even our own, in terms of their literal surface expression, and hence in terms of what is literally said or represented. To return to a theme introduced earlier (in chapter 2, section 2.4), reported or (meta)represented thoughts are "objects before the mind," and in particular before the folk-psychological mind; they are not thoughts in, or deployed by, the mind in its normal, conative, cognitive, and thus predicative mode. The Fregean-style thinking about predication was said then to be heavily influenced by the notion of thought as reported or represented thought, thought-before-the-mind, and hence in terms of its surface expression, on a par with what is literally said, and hence as a coinstantiation.

In-the-mind, however, deployed in the normal conative and cognitive mode, thoughts operate as deep predications, in communication and thinking as well. The illustration above suggested a few parameters of normal communication, such as context, shared assumptions, supporting evidence, memories, a contrast class of alternative interpretations of what is said, and so on. Deep predication in thinking works pretty much in the same way, for a very good developmental reason: predication grows out of the intended meaning or the intent/ionality of communication, as it is redesigned through word acquisition by shared naming.

Short of daydreaming and other forms of "mental ballistics," in which (surface) thoughts pop up in one's head without any particular reason and mental pedigree, most likely as coinstantiations, normal thinking as goal-directed "mental artillery" has a good deal in common with communication by intended meaning. Instead of context, thinking may have a theme; instead of being shared with a partner, assumptions are part of the theme and its background information (memories, etc.); instead of a contrast class of alternative interpretations of literal meaning, thinking usually proceeds by an implicit eliminative induction, assigning utilities and probabilities to, and settling on, some representations of a fact, situation, or possibility, as opposed to others; and so on (Bogdan 1994, chapter 7).

Deep Thoughts

One way to individuate the predicativeness of normal, goal-directed thinking is to look for the question, uncertainty, problem, or objective that drives a particular train of thoughts. That determination may identify a theme, background, and topic for the thoughts, and then the answer or solution—or whatever settles the question, uncertainty, or problem, and concludes that train of thought—would be a candidate for the comment. This is what is going on below the surface, in the main body of the iceberg—the deep predication.

The surface expression of a thought is most often a compact summary of a deep predication. It is a summary explicitly and conventionally encoded for intelligible, economical, and effective public communication, or further utilization, in public terms, in one's inference, imagination, recall, and so on. Alongside formal "transformations" that convert deep predications into their surface expressions (to borrow an idea from the theory of grammar), something like Grice's strictures on effective communication as well as Sperber's and Wilson's relevance computations may also constrain the process.

To take an example, suppose that I come to think that August is not the best time to be in Paris. If this were a popping-out-of-nowhere sort of thought (as a literal meaning), then an analysis of its minimal propositional (and nonpredicative) content in terms of something like <August&Paris&Not Good> will do quite nicely and perhaps as effectively. But this analysis will be far from sufficient, if this same thought is a tip-of-the-iceberg one resulting from a deep predication. In this latter case, my thought has a context or theme (traveling to Paris), assumptions of some sort (money, vacation time, meeting friends, and eating well), a specific topic (when to be in Paris), some utility values (what is expected from being in Paris at different times), a contrast class of alternatives (possible times, or given assumptions and utilities), and so forth. The comment itself (not in August) is the outcome of canvasing a number of facts (too many friends inexplicably behaving like the rest of the bourgeoisie and therefore gone, too many camera-heavy tourists, and, *le pire,* many restaurants closed). In any event, without this tip versus iceberg or surface versus deep picture, it would not be evident that "not in August" is a comment and hence the intended predicate, and that "the time to be in Paris" is the intended topic and hence the subject. Nor would it be evident what the *intended* force or meaning of the comment is, besides its literal reference to a month to be avoided in a certain (admittedly unique) place.

There are some further considerations that support this deep-surface analysis of predication. One is the familiar fact that what counts as the subject or topic of a thought or sentence, at which a commenting predicate is directed, can vary indefinitely in nature and complexity. It can be an object, an event, four related events, a complex scene, an idea, a theory, or what have you. This is the intended flexibility of the topic, of what we decide, or happen, to think or talk about. The same can be said about what counts as a predicate, reflecting the underlying flexibility of commenting. It is hard to see how the classical grammatical, logical, and metaphysical analyses—all surface analyses, so to speak—can account for such a flexibility without taking into account what thinkers or communicators intend to think about or communicate.

Another consideration is the intended flexibility of what gets explicitly encoded linguistically as subject and predicate, and what is presupposed in a context of thinking or communication. The explicit encodings in words are, after all, only the tip of the iceberg that individuates a complete thought or unit of communication. Recall the earlier observation that fully formed utterances are still construed by the three-year-old child as comments on topics that are visually shared with an adult. We now see that this fact may shed light on a basic and pervasive phenomenon, reaching far and deep into adult communication and thinking. The phenomenon is that the topic-comment-presupposition format is not necessarily—and actually seldom is—fully manifested or visible in the symbolically explicit surface form of an utterance or worded thought. As Bates (1976, 97) writes, "If the speaker uses his utterance as a comment upon some contextually available information and assumes that his listener can reconstruct the same relationship, then a psychological presupposition is present even if the sentence itself contains no explicit reference to that presupposition. Hence, a decision essential to every act of speaking—the choice of which elements to encode and which elements to take for granted—requires the psychological act of presupposing" (see also Sperber and Wilson 1986).

The choice of which elements to encode linguistically (or gesturally, as in sign language), how to parse them into subjects and predicates, and which elements to take for granted begins with the learning of the first words explicitly introduced by shared naming. Gradually, once in control of a vocabulary, the child is able to distance herself from perception and shared attention, and use what the interlocutor *says* as implying shared presuppositions and shared topics for predicative comments. As the child's conversation becomes more sophisticated and removed from perceptual contexts, the child develops new mental strategies of tracking the presuppositions and topics shared with an interlocutor, and also strategies of deciding which elements of an utterance to encode explicitly, and how explicitly, and which to presuppose. It is likely that explicit and communication-inspired thinking develops along the same lines.

For decades, philosophers, psycholinguists, and developmental psychologists have been familiar with the idea that linguistic predication piggybacks on the prelinguistic shoulders of the topic-comment-presupposition matrix (among others, Adamson 1995; Bates 1976; Bruner 1983; Cook Wilson 1926; Gibson 2004; Hobson 1993; Ramsey 1925; Tomasello 1999). Equally familiar has been the idea that beneath almost any descriptive utterance or sentence, there is an underlying topic-comment-presupposition format—the iceberg that does the real work (Clark and Clark 1977; Dretske 1972; Sperber and Wilson 1986; see also Bogdan 1987, 1994). In a pioneering work of real-life epistemology, Fred Dretske (1969) also argued that visual perception works in an incremental manner, which when embedded in a larger cognitive (and I would add, often communication-shaped) envelope, approximates the topic-comment-presupposition format; and the same seems to be true of deliberate and effortful memory recall (Loftus 1980, chapter 5). The general point, then, is that deep predications reach far into various domains of deliberate, conscious, and goal-directed mentation (Bogdan 1994).

What this book has endeavored to add to this body of work is the notion that the topic-comment-presupposition format of communication turns linguistically predicative under the impact, and in the matrix, of word acquisition by shared naming, when this format develops an intended descriptive force and an intended directedness of the comment, turned predicate, at the topic, turned subject.

With the strictly developmental argument of this book (truly and finally) over, it is time to tie up some loose ends, draw some implications, consider some questions and objections, and speculate on the historical origins of the developmental assembly of predication. Thus, the next and concluding chapter.

III Epilogue

6 Implications and Speculations

It is time now to loosen shoes, tie, mind, and tongue, and indulge in some evolutionary and neuropsychological guesses about why, how, and even when the social ontogenesis of predication might have started. The reader who is ready or curious to go beyond the developmental argument of the previous chapters is invited to join for the ride. It should be bumpy, often in the dark (more than before, that is), and at times appropriately irritating—in short, fun. Along the way, some main themes of this book get reviewed from new angles.

Section 6.1 develops the earlier suggestion that predication may have started as an accidental by-product of the evolution of more basic adaptations of human ontogeny. Section 6.2 probes the work of the brain that this accident may have brought about, and section 6.3 wonders when the evolutionary accident may have occurred. Finally, section 6.4 looks back at some debatable claims made in this book, asks some critical questions, and ventures some further implications.

6.1 Incidental Predicator

The creative intellect of adults is an incidental effect of selection for high intellectual capacity in juvenile humans
—Richard Alexander, "How Humans Evolved"

Predication is at the heart of conscious and symbolically explicit human thinking, which in turn is at the heart of such intellectual activities as deliberation, reflective planning, theoretical imagination, abstract and hypothetical reasoning, and reflexive thinking. The implication, then, to paraphrase Alexander's motto for this section, would be that the adult intellect may be an incidental effect of selection for predication and other early faculties in juvenile humans. Yet according to earlier chapters, the predication competence itself looks like an incidental effect of selection for still other, even more basic, and earlier ontogenetic adaptations, such as physiological and psychological coregulation, meaning-exchanging communication, coreferential triangulations, shared attention, and word acquisition. These latter adaptations develop initially in contexts as well as for reasons that have little, if anything, to do with predication, or indeed with cognition in general and conscious and symbolic thinking in particular.

Each step on the ontogenetic staircase to communicative meaning, word acquisition by shared naming, and predication reflects the interplay between the goal-oriented and imperative dispositions and thoughts of the young child and the coregulatory, communicational, and word-acquisition challenges the child faces in relation to adults. The child's sense of meaning was shown to emerge from coregulation and recognition of adult mental intent, a sense of coreferential intent from the joint communicational engagement of shared targets of interest, and the capacity for symbolic predication from the shared-attention contexts of deliberate and explicit introduction of words by shared naming. These early acquisitions, conducive to predication, are mostly dated and result first in dated interpersonal and communicational adaptations. They do not have the *initial* functions of cognitive representation, let alone the cognitive form of representation embodied in linguistic predication.

These considerations favor the conjecture that the ability to predicate does not mature out of a single and dedicated genetic blueprint. The lack of a genetic source (and it seems, the absence of a brain site specialized in predication) and the human uniqueness of predication speak against the notion of a gradual phylogenetic process of natural selection of a predication competence among primates or, as we shall see, even early humans. Nor does it seem likely that children develop the ability to predicate on their own, through learning, imitation, or some other sort of induction from examples. It was noted earlier that what young children hear (or otherwise register) from adults is most often a simplified baby talk (or baby signing) whose predicative structure, if any, is unlikely to be discerned, or when they hear normal speech, they may at best register its coinstantiative (not predicative) parsing.

Indeed, if the cognitive challenge facing young children were to identify and combine representations of objects, properties, and relations, they could just as well develop only thematic coinstantiations, which is what I think Bermudez (2003) has shown about some animal species, and which may also be true of children younger than nine to twelve months. The children's first words and the one- or two-word constructions seem indeed to have coinstantiative semantics. The coinstantiations are made of expressive as well as vaguely referential words, which children pick up without much, if any, deliberate and explicit adult instruction (Adamson 1995; Bates 1976; P. Bloom 2000; Tomasello 2003). As I speculate in section 6.3 below, such a holophrastic language of thematic coinstantiations may well have been used by premodern humans, prior to the evolution of deliberate and explicit parental practices of word introduction by shared naming.

If the predication competence is neither innate nor formed through individual experience, what could explain its formation? An answer is ventured in the next section.

6.2 Assembly Work

This book has argued for a developmental pattern that is more akin to a gradual *assembly* during and through which several of the young child's diverse abilities and dispositions, with initially diverse functions, are recruited, redirected, bundled together, and routinized, particularly under adult pressure and guidance, as ontogenetic adaptations that respond to the specific interpersonal and communicational challenges of early childhood. The developmental literature cites—and debates—many instances when the behavioral dispositions and biases of young children are reorganized and/or given new functions under adult culture in general, and explicit prompting and guidance in particular.

Adult Redesign

A much-discussed adult redesign practice is *scaffolding*—generally understood as an adult's effort to structure a context of interaction with a child in order to simplify and guide the child's grasp and performance of a task (Adamson 1995; Bruner 1983; Rogoff 1990; Vygotsky 1981). Scaffolding is particularly effective in teaching children how to handle tools and other cultural gadgets, and how to behave in culturally canonical ways (Tomasello 1999). There are other sorts of adult practices that redesign the child's dispositions and abilities—ones that are less complex or artificial than scaffolding, but no less potent and consequential. Thus, Vasudevi Reddy (1991) suggests that humor initially develops in the child's mind in social contexts through violations of canonical expectations of child-adult interactions, such as giving and taking. At around eight to nine months of age, infants notice that a noncanonical behavior provokes a humorous reaction in an adult, which is often a deliberate reinterpretation of the event, so they repeat the behavior solely with humorous intent (I still do it). A disposition for humor is eventually installed by way of adult reaction and reinterpretation (with mixed results, I should say). The same pattern seems to work in the case of teasing.

There are other examples as well. Lev Vygotsky (1981, 161) thought that adults respond to the infant's grasping movement by reinterpreting and ultimately redesigning it as pointing to a target (for a different view, see Bates 1976; Werner and Kaplan 1963). Vygotsky also thought that young children's attention becomes focused and voluntary under adult verbal direction, as does self-regulation. Crying is another example of adult redesign of a behavioral disposition. Crying is widely thought to manifest an initial disposition to express distress, as a built-in reaction to an internal state, and also as a formula to attract the mother's attention and secure her proximity (Bates 1979, 34). At some point in infancy, the mother begins to reinterpret crying as meaning something like "Aha, you want this!" where "this" could be an object, event, or action, and the child comes to associate crying with wanting something (Lock 1980, 52). The mother (or some adult) thus redesigns an initial physiological response into an intentional act directed at something or other.

Both the grabbing-to-pointing and crying-to-expressing-wanting metamorphoses may be thought of as adult *intent/ionalization* of a child's disposition or propensity, to coin a term commensurate with the dual sense of intent/ionality introduced earlier (chapter 4, section 4.3). Simplistically phrased, "intent/ionalization" means a deliberate adult effort to endow a child's disposition and behavior, which initially were not related to a target (had no aboutness) and were not intended to be (had no intent), with an intent related to some target. Without adult redesign, crying, for example, could conceivably have remained what it was initially, and what it was probably selected for: namely, a propensity to express distress or a need for attention.

To the extent that shared attention marks a deliberate and sustained effort of adults to engage children in sharing intents to corefer to targets of mutual interest, it too can be construed as a form of adult intent/ionalization of the child's propensity to communicate. In shared attention, the child recognizes the adult's intent to corefer. The mutual recognition of intents to communicate, originating earlier in bilateral communication, and the mutual sense of shared target may act as a bridge (so to speak) that enables the child to acquire a sense of her own referring as mental directedness to a target. This move from (shared) intent to (shared) target directedness or aboutness, effected in shared attention, does not appear to develop innately and spontaneously in the child's mind (Adamson 1995; Hobson 1993; but for a different view of a modular shared attention that matures endogenously, see Baron-Cohen 1995). The evidence cited in the previous chapter in connection with shared naming suggests a deliberate adult effort to turn the child's intent to share a target into an explicit sense of coreferring.

Assembly Solutions

The young child faces many and diverse interpersonal, communicational, and cultural challenges generated by adults and their cultural world. The child comes equipped with innate dispositions and abilities, particularly for coregulative and imperative communication, and probably some abilities for making sense of other minds—what I called the roots of predication. The child meets some of the challenges by spontaneously assembling solutions out of such innate dispositions and abilities, without the solutions themselves being genetically programmed. The detection of meaning in infant-adult communication, along with the associative learning of the first words and some forms of joint triangulation, such as social referencing, may be internally and thus spontaneously yet not genetically developed solutions. The solutions may emerge in a pieces-falling-into-place sort of pattern, especially if the pattern is sufficiently constrained by adults and their culture, as it generally is in early childhood.

Bates (1979, 17) provides a good illustration of this kind of solution: the example of eating with one's hands. It is rather unlikely that the flexible use of hands was selected for eating, as opposed to throwing or carrying things, or climbing trees. Since available, the hands get recruited for eating. Although hand-feeding employs innate resources within an innately determined range of actions, it need not be based on any *specific* and *dedicated* genetic mechanism. Given the task of eating, and the anatomical and neural organization of the hands, the solution of hand-feeding is so probable that no further genetic specialization is needed. Nor does hand-feeding have to be learned or trained, although it could and often is. (How else to explain that most Europeans eat with the two hands visibly on the table, and most Americans with one invisibly under the table?) A child left alone or in the wild will soon stumble on the solution without outside help.

Other assembly solutions, equally nongenetic, may not be possible without deliberate adult redesign. In the developmental saga of predication, shared naming is a prime example of adult-assisted solutions. What is important to note about these assembly solutions and particularly the adult-assisted ones is that once mastered and routinized, the solutions no longer bear witness to how they were arrived at. To use an old metaphor, the ladder that got the child's mind to that level of competence is discarded, once it did its job. Older children and adults no longer represent meaning-conveying intent in terms of affective looks exchanged bilaterally with adults, as infants do, or word reference in the coreferential terms of shared attention, as do twelve- to eighteen-month-olds.

Here is an apt parallel of a soon-discarded cultural ladder to a new form of representation. Children are genetically primed to recognize the phonetics of any language (initial disposition). This recognition soon shrinks to the phonetics of the particular language spoken around them. Later, after mastering the alphabet (a late cultural acquisition both in evolution and development), children come to recognize the sound system of their language in terms of the alphabet, not of its initial phonetics. Thus, for instance, English-speaking children think that there are more units in "pitch" than in "rich," even though phonetically there is no discernible difference (Olson 1994, 85). The assimilation of the alphabet redesigns the initial phonetic recognition by inserting (nongenetically) its contribution into the sound system of the language. The alphabetized child and adult no longer represent the first steps to the culturally redesigned phonetics of their language.

Suppose that the predication competence is assembled along the lines suggested in this section and documented in earlier chapters. What, inside the child's head, would explain the possibility of such an assembly? The following is an answer that I find rather plausible.

Neural Plasticity for Assembly

There is a familiar idea in evolutionary theory that a lengthy ontogeny increases adaptability by allowing offspring more time, energy, and brain flexibility to adjust to highly complex environments, and in the human case, dynamic and arms-race spawning cultures (Bjorklund and Pellegrini 2002; Chisholm 1988). This evolutionary idea is echoed in neuroscience, where the thinking is that by retarding or extending the rate of somatic development, neural structures are given more time to grow and differentiate, and thus be affected by the developmental milieu. This neuroscientific conjecture is often taken to imply that neural plasticity is selected for *learning*. That may be true about mental inductions, such as accumulating information as well as acquiring behavioral and cultural routines, but probably less true about developing mental abilities, such as communicating meaningfully (à la Grice), acquiring words, predicating, thinking abstractly, imagining counterfactually, and so on. After all, most animal species learn in the former sense but do not develop the latter abilities, not even nonhuman primates with a lengthy and human-reared childhood.

In the case of the child's development of mental abilities like those examined in this work, neural plasticity may mean something else. It may mean an evolved readiness to *assemble* task-specific ontogenetic adaptations out of prior adaptations, other abilities, and dispositions whose initial tasks—and reasons of being—may have been different. This is how I read the claim that neural development generates redundant and variable synaptic typologies that provide the raw material of epigenesis, so that neural selection, mostly through local and dated pressures, can favor the preservation or stabilization of those synapses that have functional significance in a particular environment at a particular time (Changeux 1985; Dennett 1991). The implication I see is that many, if not most, of the interpersonal, cultural, and as a result, mental ontogenetic adaptations of the young child are outcomes of *selection for an assembly ready neural plasticity*.

This assemblist reading of neural plasticity during development fits nicely with the story told in this book. Adaptations for coregulation joined forces with adaptations for face and emotion reading, and resulted in adaptations for bilateral intersubjective communication; the latter joined forces with abilities for imperative communication to produce child-world-adult protodeclaratives, which later were bundled with joint triangulations and shared attention into topic-comment ostensive proto-predications, and so on, along the ontogenetic staircase to word acquisition and predication. The universality and regimented schedule of these mental acquisitions suggests a tight scheduling rather than variable learning. If that is the case, then the question is what could explain such universality and scheduling.

One possibility, of course, is genetic programming. Yet as noted on earlier occasions, the abilities for handling (possibly) meaning and (certainly) word coreference by shared naming and predication do not seem to be innate—or more exactly, do not point to specific and functionally dedicated genetic bases from where they mature as mental modules. As far as I know, there is no evidence of specific brain mechanisms for recognizing and handling meaning or word coreference by shared naming, or managing predications. None of these abilities seems to be domain specific and cognitively impenetrable, as mental modules are thought to be. Nor do there seem to be identifiable deficits in their exercise, due to old age or brain impairments. So what would be the evolutionary alternative to straightforward genetic programming?

Recall that the mental assembly of intended meaning, word coreference by shared naming, and particularly predication was said to result from the child's ontogenetic adaptations to two sorts of pressures and constraints: immaturity, helplessness, and adult dependence, on the one hand; and the adult initiation of the child into world-directed communication, language, and culture, on the other hand. The former may explain the opportunities for the assembly of *specific* innate dispositions and ontogenetic adaptations into the predication competence, but seems less apt to explain the *general* underlying readiness for such assembly, its historical stimulus, and particularly its ontogenetic pattern. After all, long immaturity, helplessness, and adult dependence are also conditions of the offspring of higher mammals and nonhuman primates, though to a lesser degree, and also of hominids and premodern humans to a degree comparable to modern children (Boyd and Silk 1997; Tomasello and Call 1997). Yet modern humans seem to be the only predicators and intellectual thinkers.

It is, I suspect, the *adult contribution*, interpersonal and cultural—in the form of interactions, pressures, guidance, and initiation into language and culture—that, *back in evolutionary history*, may have forced the brains of modern human children into novel and unique ontogenetic adaptations, and a pattern of assembling them into new competencies, including explicit word acquisition by shared naming and predication. The latter in turn opened up new ontogenetic trajectories leading up to the human intellect. The archaeological record, incomplete as it is, suggests that the modern human mind may have evolved rather recently and perhaps speedily (Boyd and Silk 1997; Mithen 1996). This recent evolution may have started with a cascade of ontogenetic adaptations brought about by a relatively recent revolution in human parenting. This is the speculative idea I sketch next.

6.3 Way Back When

Revolution in Parenting

The adult initiation strategies begin with (what may be called) the "intuitive parenting" stance that human adults spontaneously adopt toward children. There is a mystery about where such an intuitive parenting comes from, yet it appears to be universal, though culturally rather than biologically induced (Adamson 1995, 70–71). Whence two historical questions: What brought about such intuitive parenting, with its initiation, intervention, and redesign policies; and when?

The answer to the first question could be a revolution in human parenting. It may have been generated by a mutual *sexual selection* for novel forms of parenting: males favoring females who spend more time and effort in close emotional and pedagogical contact with their children, and females favoring males who appreciate, protect, and support this parental investment, and even get involved in the new relationship to children (Boyd and Silk 1997, chapter 7; Sterelny and Fitness 2003; see also Bogdan 2005). The parenting innovations may have involved longer and subtler bilateral exchanges of experiences and vocalizations, including the emergence of baby talk or motherese, which all sharpened the infant's ability to detect the adult's mental intent and attention, and thus a sense of other minds, more helpful ways of later triangulating targets of shared interest, and still later, cleverer ways of texturing and scaffolding the contexts in which vocalizations and pointings are connected with items to be named, and so on.

Assuming that as a result of these parental novelties some children were performing better mentally, parental pressures may have initiated and fueled an escalating arms race, whereby the children's new acquisitions were met with new tasks to perform, which forced new ontogenetic adaptations facing again new tasks, and so forth. Confronted with this arms race, the minds of young children may have responded in (at least) two ways. Their innate biases and mechanisms may have acted as evaluators and filters of which parental innovations were assimilable and which weren't, leading up to a mutually adjusted coevolutionary equilibrium in the scheduling, rhythm, and degree of difficulty of the (mostly) linguistic and cultural challenges thrown at the child. Another response, parallel to the first, may have been the neural plasticity and readiness for assembling new mental skills discussed in the previous section.

There is plenty of evidence of selection for the plasticity of developmental programs in many animal species as a result of variable pressures in the environment. For example, there is a species of fish (Labroides dimidiata) whose little ones begin as female, but then turn male when they become the largest in the group; different diets transform a female ant into a worker or a queen; and less food slows down the development and size of most organisms, just as less light slows down the development of many plants. In none of these cases is the developmental response learned. How could it be? The disposition to develop flexibly is selected for in the form of genetically based developmental *strategies* (Tooby and Cosmides 1992; Williams 1966). The cultural environment of human children is surely the most variable and dynamic in the living world, and rather unpredictable from the genome's perspective. The skills needed to handle a cultural environment are so diverse (emotional, social, communicational, linguistic, and cognitive) and their interplay so intricate that one would expect nature to settle for a selection for *flexible strategies of assembly* of such skills and other faculties rather than for genetically prefabricated solutions.

The selection itself may well have been of the Baldwinian or genetic-assimilation sort (Boyd and Silk 1997; Deacon 1997; Dennett 1991, 1995). Suppose that, way back, some young children may have luckily assembled the right responses to the parental innovations that led to meaning-conveying communication, a sense of coreference, word acquisition by shared naming, and predication. More and more parents then increasingly favored these assembled improvisations, thus increasing the selection pressures on young children generally, until biological luck had it that some children assimilated genetically the readiness to assemble all these predication-building abilities, perhaps along the ontogenetic staircase suggested in this book. The rest is history.

The mental improvisations of young human-reared apes in captivity, which is mostly a cultural captivity, offer some retrospective hints as to how this historical process might have unfolded. Think of Kanzi, the bonobo who learned alone how to use lexigrams to communicate with people (Savage-Rumbaugh and Lewin 1996), or think of the apes who learn a sort of target-directed pointing. Since few captive apes develop such skills (the lexigram-using performance of Kanzi's mother, for instance, was much inferior, despite intense training), and since all apes are capable of learning, one can reasonably infer that Kanzi and the pointing apes were somehow able to recruit and assemble the right skills that initially may have had different (selected) functions in the wild. Imagine now a (rather improbable) future scenario in which many generations of such young captive apes face the strong pressure of the human preference for such assembled improvisations as responses to symbols and culture. At some point in time, luck might genetically install in some young captive apes a readiness to assemble—perhaps along an ontogenetic staircase—new skills that respond to the unusual tasks imposed on them. As adults in a symbolic and cultural environment, those lucky fictional apes will outperform the unlucky ones and come to dominate the group or population. Lest we forget, human children do *begin* their lives as young primates in cultural captivity, and did so for hundreds of millennia.

This take on the parentally induced genetic readiness to assemble novel abilities may help evaluate a debate about the extent to which active adult intervention and redesign (scaffolding, tutoring, deliberate intent/ionalization, and even shared attention) are actually needed by children in order to climb the ontogenetic staircase to word acquisition, predication, and other mental competencies. The evidence is said to be fairly inconclusive and controversial (Adamson 1995). I noted that children learn their first words without adult help and that shared attention is thought not to be so decisive in word acquisition (P. Bloom 2000). At best, it looks like adult assistance improves performance—for example, children learn more words with shared attention than without (Tomasello 1999, 2003)—rather than shaping a competence. Finally, children are known to develop their own versions of simple languages—say, pidgin or the gestural code of the deaf Nicaraguan children—without adult presence, let alone assistance (Bickerton 1990).

I do not think these considerations speak against the argument of this chapter and the whole book. On the contrary, they support it, for at least two reasons. One, just outlined in the last few paragraphs, is that the readiness to assemble abilities along an ontogenetic staircase is a matter of competence or developmental design, selected a *long time ago*, and not a matter of actual performance and experiential input in individual cases of development. Actual performance may vary considerably, and input may be minimal or even absent altogether, without necessarily affecting the developmental design itself. This is a cognitive-scientific truth first intuited by Plato: one can have a competence, yet exercise it poorly, deviantly, or not at all. Thus, the second reason: if the child *is genetically primed* to assemble adult-sensitive or interpersonal mental abilities that lead up to a sense of communicative meaning, word coreference by shared naming, and predication, according to a well-scheduled pattern, then we can expect the child to initiate the assembly even with *minimal* input and assistance. Trevarthen's idea of the innate virtual other may reflect this anticipative interpersonal adaptation of early childhood. Normal performance at each major step on the ontogenetic staircase may suffer, often dramatically, or be delayed if input and assistance are minimal—if, for example, the virtual other is not sufficiently actualized. The evidence on this score seems solid (Adamson 1995; P. Bloom 2000; Tomasello 2003). The same can be said about congenital handicaps, particularly autism and blindness (Hobson 1993).

The evolutionary hypothesis about a revolution in parenting that may have led to the ontogenetic staircase to predication is about what human adults did a *long while ago*, which resulted in a redesign of the coregulatory, communicational, naive-psychological, and word-acquisition equipment of the young child. It is *not* about what subsequent generations of parents and other adults do every day in the presence of children. Yet again, it is a fact that children tend to perform poorly if parents and adults do not do well in assisting and guiding them on the staircase, or if children are impaired in their relation to adults. This fact is a firm indication that the children's predication-building ontogenetic adaptations and assembly strategies are socially sensitive to adults as a matter of evolved genetic design.

To recap, suppose that a revolution in parenting actually did start the ontogenetic progression to predication. Suppose also that it pressured the young minds into evolving a neural readiness for assembling the right ontogenetic adaptations. Suppose finally that the innate biases, dispositions, and adaptations of the child's mind filtered in the assimilable adult interventions and their timing, while filtering out the wrong versions and timings, thereby generating a coevolutionary adjustment that eventuated in something like the ontogenetic staircase to explicit and shared word acquisition and predication. If these suppositions are not too wide of the mark, the next question we (or at least the brave ones among us) may want to ask—or (in my case) cannot help but ask—is the historical when. (Good luck.)

When?

Historical estimates about the origin of and reasons for biological traits are tricky enough. Those about mental faculties are much harder, hotly debated, and constantly revised. Despite the misgivings of many philosophers and cognitive scientists, I think the exercise is as worthy as speculations in cosmology about the history of the universe or in physics about the deep-down stringlike multiverse composition of the world. (The string theory is said to have so far no conclusive evidence for its hypotheses. Yet string theorists are treated more respectfully, and are probably better paid or at least better grant supported, than are evolutionary archaeologists of the mind.) Informed speculation widens our theoretical horizon and tests the coherence of what we know so far in distinct but interacting domains of science. With this in mind, and if read with reasonable approximation and healthy skepticism, some comparative archaeological data seem to support the developmental picture drawn in this book (Boyd and Silk 1997; Deacon 1997; Donald 1991; Mithen 1996; Tomasello and Call 1997).

Perhaps the most telling piece of evidence is that the human brain may have reached its present size and possibly its manifest cognitive capacities some 250,000 years ago, if not earlier, yet some of its uniquely modern activities, which left some archaeological traces such as complex tool making, art, rituals, burial, and religion, emerged much later, perhaps only about 50,000 to 75,000 years ago. There is a consensus in the literature that the latter activities draw on higher mental functions or (what we may call) the abilities of the *intellect*, including advanced linguistic communication, imagination, reflective planning, and deliberation, introspection, and reflexive thinking (Mithen 1996). These intellectual faculties draw on the prior abilities to represent meaning and word reference as well as to predicate. So we can call the latter abilities and predication in particular the incubator of the intellect. The implication, then, is that at least some of the incubator abilities—in particular predication—may have evolved sometime close to 50,000 to 75,000 years ago, perhaps as a result of the parental revolution evoked earlier, the arms race it spawned, and the resulting ontogenetic staircase.

Backing this conjecture are two neurobiological considerations. One, already noted, is that neither most of the incubator abilities nor the resulting intellectual faculties seem to have functionally dedicated, brain localized, and genetically expressed mechanisms. They are not modules, in other words. And if most of these incubator abilities develop more like predication, in an assembly-like manner, they (too) are unlikely to have evolved incrementally by natural selection. The other consideration is that the basic *modular* mechanisms of the modern human brain are conjectured to have evolved much earlier than the intellect—perhaps between 250,000 and 1,000,000 years ago, if not even earlier (Boyd and Silk 1997; Mithen 1996). I read these data and considerations to suggest that an *assembly* process, along the lines indicated earlier, was involved in the *late* evolution of the incubator abilities and the intellect they made possible.

Even the highly uncertain and wildly conflicting estimates of the evolution of language do not seem to contradict this reading. A primitive, prepredicative, and coinstantiative language would have had almost as much use for gestural, phonetic, and conceptual resources as its modern predicative successor. This is why such resources may have emerged as early as premodern humans or even hominids. Prior to the modern revolution in parenting, such a primitive protolanguage was probably holophrastic, employing one- or two-word constructions, on the model of thematic coinstantiations and the child's first words (Bickerton 1990; Wray 2000). These protowords and coinstantiative constructions may have been acquired through associations and contextual clues, and used mostly as imperative signals. They probably had a rough semantics, and in the absence of predication, were involved in rather minimal, if any, syntactic computations, although as noted before, a fairly complex coinstantiative grammar need not be excluded.

There is a possible parallel here with the story of the (modern) child's first words, acquired around six months and later (chapter 5, section 5.2). As Derek Bickerton (2004) notes, the speech of children younger than two is a highly probable approximation of a premodern protolanguage. If that was the case historically, then my analysis suggests that the communication, language, and thinking of premodern humans were not yet predicative, although they may have been minimally propositional and coinstantiative.

A primitive, prepredicative, and coinstantiative language might conceivably coexist with an underlying language of thought and even a grammar (a point made abstractly in chapter 2, section 2.2). Grammar may have evolved (much) earlier than 50,000 to 75,000 years ago, given its universality and the onset of the human diaspora about 90,000 years ago (Bickerton 2000, 2004). Yet grammar may have remained underemployed and coinstantiative for a long time, and hence unemployed predicatively, particularly if it did not start as language dedicated and grew instead out of some precursor abilities with other initial functions, such as motor behavior (Arbib 2005) or protothinking (Wray 2000), or else was language dedicated from the outset, but evolved slowly and incrementally (Pinker and Bloom 1990). As frequently noted throughout this book, the "is" of coinstantiation can handle many grammatical tasks without actually predicating anything of anything.

If any of these hypotheses turns out to be right, it should not cause too much surprise to learn that it may have been the evolving grammar that responded adaptively to the *prior* presence of a predication competence in young minds rather than the other way around, as most linguists, philosophers, and cognitive scientists (including most of my professional friends) believe. In general, once human ontogeny took the relatively recent and dramatic turn to predication, possibly triggered by a parental revolution and the adaptive responses of the children's minds, one may expect the predicative advances in communication and word acquisition to have generated new pressures on as well as opportunities for the other resources of language, grammar included, and the human mind in general.

The moral of the story, then, is that in both human evolution and human ontogeny, the emergence of predication is a radical turning point to the extent that it begins to redesign imagistic, associative, and imperative minds into intellects. The redesign itself results from a socially driven child-adult-world venture involved progressively in coregulation, communication, and the acquisition of words by shared naming during early childhood.

6.4 Retrospective

This concluding section reviews the highlights of the main story, as a recapitulation and also a background for considering further questions and implications.

The Developmental Argument

The leading idea pursued in this book has been that the child's mental scheme that represents word coreference, introduced by adults through shared naming, becomes an incubator and template for the mental scheme of predication. The precursors of the naming-representing scheme itself are assembled gradually, since infancy, out of several components, chief among them being the young child's sense of bilateral meaning (from coregulative communication), the intent/ionality of other minds (from a sense of other minds and later naive psychology), the world-directed protodeclaratives (from imperative communication), and the sense of coreferential intent and coreferential triangulation (manifested chiefly in shared attention). The protopredicative scheme installed ostensively in the child's mind by shared naming in turn reshapes her communicative thoughts into full-fledged predicative structures.

This ontogenetic progression toward predication follows a central pattern of gradual initiation into, and then redesign of, the child's topic-comment-presupposition format of communication. This format is the ur-matrix of predication, the mother of all predications. Its ontogenesis goes through two major phases: prelinguistic and linguistic. The earliest coregulative communication is an initiation into a sort of commentariat without a topic, whereby the comment first emerges as an expression of intent to produce a mental effect in an addressee, and be so recognized, by displaying an addressor's inner condition, such as an emotion, interest, or feeling. The comment, expressing an intent to convey a state of mind, is the bilateral and nonreferential forerunner of communicative meaning, later condensed into an explicit predicate.

On the parallel track of imperative communication, the protodeclarative version focuses on an egocentric and not yet shared topic as external target toward which the child directs the adult's attention. The result is joint (but not yet coreferential and hence incomplete) triangulations in which the child-adult exchange of expressive comments is still bilateral, with the external topic only implicit in a shared context. Shared attention completes the joint triangulation of a topic through mutually recognized, topic-directed, and partner-addressed comments. The joint triangulation turns coreferential and fully shared. This is because, for the first time, shared attention provides the child with a sense of someone's coreferential intent. With the onset of shared naming, this sense enables the child to recognize and use conventionally symbolic reference, and in particular word reference.

The topic-comment-presupposition format can thus be regarded as the main ontogenetic matrix in which are assembled the mental schemes for representing meaning, coreference, and predication. This assembly work is done during the process—and as a consequence—of upgrading and retooling the communicational skills of the child in order to facilitate the assimilation of the vocabulary of a natural language. Predicative thinking is, on this analysis, a by-product of the development of communication in general, and its topic-comment-presupposition format and role in language acquisition in particular. This format was also shown to continue to animate and organize predicative communication and thinking beyond childhood.

The Philosophical Argument

The topic-comment-presupposition format is one of the three critical P-dimensions of predication, the other two being its intended descriptiveness and the intended predicate-to-subject directedness. These dimensions were shown not to be inherent in, and not to grow out of, the possession of thematic categories—objects, properties, agents, actions, and so on—and the logical and grammatical algorithms of a language, whether mental or natural. The P-dimensions are not present in the classical but minimal notion of proposition, understood in terms of the S-dimensions. The P-dimensions were also shown to distinguish predication from such faux candidates as thematic coinstantiation and even syntactic constructions of such coinstantiations. Contrary to mainstream philosophical wisdom, possessing conceptually and even formally structured propositional thoughts is not yet possessing predicative thoughts.

Philosophers have long worried about the mystery of the unity of the predication (its being more than the sum of its parts). A mind—animal or human—can link the representation of an object and a property under appropriate categories without necessarily predicating the latter of the former. A human mind (alone) can even interpose the copula "is" between those two representations and even think that this is how the linkage in question is achieved linguistically, and still not predicate. The missing link is the intended predicate-to-subject directedness, whereby the subject is understood as fixing the topic and the predicate as a comment intently and explicitly directed at the topic. The developmental story told in this book is mostly one of how and when children assemble the resources for such an understanding.

Questions-and-Answers Period

I expect many of the positions taken in this book and many of the arguments that support them to raise doubts, questions, and objections, some of which are considered and answered below. Neither the earlier sections and chapters nor the answers below aim at certainty and closure. What they aim at is a healthy brainstorming and perhaps some new avenues for inquiry.

No Shared Naming, No Predication? As noted in the previous section, the connection between shared naming and predication, and thus the entire pattern of assembly of the predication competence, may have evolved tens of millennia ago as a likely outcome of a parenting revolution. As a result, the child enters the world with innate expectations and probably mental schemes for shared attention, possibly even shared naming, and a virtual other in coregulation and communication. The maturation of these expectations and mental schemes could in principle enable the child to understand word reference in patterns conducive to predication, even when adults engage in little shared attention and shared naming. But given the lack of sufficient stimuli, the child's resulting performances may be poorer in these conditions and the whole development slower.

Could a totally isolated child, without any adults around, but otherwise normal mentally, think and communicate predicatively? Not likely, I guess, if the child has no way of acquiring the vocabulary of a language, whether spoken or gestural. One needs an acoustic or visual representation of the word or sign reference relation to graduate to predication. Even though endowed with the expectations and schemes just noted, the isolated child's thinking would most likely remain coinstantiative and so would his communication, if he ever develops it, past the critical age. Missing in this case are not the innate predispositions and schemes to assemble the predication competence but rather the concrete props—words, gestures, looks, and so on—that help trigger and implement the assembly.

Why Not Straightforward Innateness? Why couldn't the predication competence be simply innate, with its own genetic mechanisms—for example, as part of the design of a language of thought or even the syntax of a natural language—and mature on its own?

It could, of course, but it is unlikely, in light of earlier arguments. It is much more likely that coinstantiation, often confused with predication, matures out of innate mechanisms, as noted in the discussion of animal and perceptual predication (chapter 2, sections 2.3 and 2.5). But coinstantiation, of course, is not predication.

Unlike the S-abilities, which could be straightforwardly innate, the P-abilities—responsible for intended descriptiveness, topic-comment-presupposition format, and intended predicate-to-subject directedness—seem much less likely to be innate and much more likely to be assembled, as argued, out of several pieces (coregulation, forms of communication, word acquisition by shared naming, and so on). The assembly itself seems to be (mostly) innately paced, probably by regulative genes, because the contributing pieces themselves are outcomes of vital but mostly dated ontogenetic adaptations. So if the predication competence can be said to be innate, it is in an indirect and convoluted way, possibly thanks to regulative genes operating on the structural genes responsible for the innate biases and schemes mentioned earlier.

Language versus Thought? How does the present account of predication bear on the language versus thought debate? Which side does it take?

It takes both sides, but rather dialectically, I would say. On the one hand, it allows for nonlinguistic and nonpredicative animal and infant thinking, possibly of the coinstantiative and minimally propositional sort. In this sense, nonpredicative, coinstantiative thinking would be independent of and prior to natural language, both phylogenetically and ontogenetically. On the other hand, the present account suggests that predicative thinking is language dependent, not in the popular sense that it is inherent in the structures and modus operandi of a natural language, but rather in the sense that the mental scheme for predication develops out of a prior mental scheme for the reference of words acquired by shared naming.

It doesn't follow, however, that we always think predicatively in language. Once the predication competence is in place, we could conceivably predicate instances of properties of instances of objects, or instances of actions of instances of agents, through images or concept applications without the mediation of linguistic structures. If at all possible, such nonlinguistic predications must be rather simple, since words alone seem capable of networking a rich variety of concepts or images. Yet again, even if possible, such simple nonlinguistic predications would employ mental schemes that are the result of the prior acquisition of words by shared naming.

Could a Language Be Just Coinstantiative? Yes, it could—just think of the predicate calculus that may actually reflect the design of a language of thought, if such a beast actually exists. Or think of various computational and programming languages, all coinstantiative, as far as I can tell. Artificial intelligence simulations of human language and thinking may have been so far only coinstantiative. But these sorts of languages would not even come close to a normal natural language, to the extent that the latter evolved precisely to accommodate and take advantage of the presence of a predication competence in the minds of its speakers, as I speculated earlier. In other words, there will be many types of constructions and hence rules in a natural language, such as cleft constructions (e.g., "it was he [i.e., me] who proposed this unusual account of predication"), that respond specifically to predicative and particularly topic-comment and not coinstantiative structures.

Coinstantiation versus Predication? Is the difference between coinstantiative and predicative thoughts actually so important? And if so, why?

I think the difference is very important. I hope I explained in what sense it is and why in the first two chapters. But let me try another angle. I noted in earlier chapters that animal or infant thoughts probably coinstantiate the observed conjunction or succession of thematically categorized items, such as objects, properties, relations, agents, actions, and so on. Such coinstantiation is likely to be automatic or reflex, mostly in perceptual and memory judgments, when certain categories are activated by sensory or memory inputs.

In contrast, predicative thoughts initially are deliberately and consciously intended by the young child—or so perceived by the young child when adults predicate—to call attention to the fact that a comment, expressed by a predicate word, is directed at a topic, which is the referent of a subject word. This is how the whole thing started. The account of predicative thinking (at the end of chapter 5) suggests that despite becoming later a routine affair, predication operates normally as part of some goal-directed thinking or communication, and reflects a mental initiative rather than a reflex automatism. In short, predicative thoughts are under conscious mental control, whereas coinstantiative thoughts need not be.

This is not to deny that with developmental advances in cognition, language mastery, and communication, and increasingly its own routine work, predicative thinking can operate without much effort or deliberation, and may even generate predicative thoughts randomly or spontaneously. We should also allow for the possibility that many of our thoughts, particularly those close to perception and mental imagery, may look predicative, when examined reflectively, but are actually minimally propositional, as recognitional coinstantiations, when exercised spontaneously.

Predication and Consciousness? Does the practice of predication, as analyzed here, require consciousness? And are predicative thoughts and utterances normally conscious?

The questions are too complex to be answered here and quickly, but I think the answers are likely yes and yes, for several reasons. First, it is hard to see how the deliberate mental intent of *directing* a comment as predicate to a topic as subject can succeed unconsciously. Second, one had better be conscious in order to decide what to encode explicitly in a predication and what to leave as presupposition; the same is true on the comprehension side, in understanding someone else's predication. Third, the goal-directed, mental artillery sort of thinking, which normally underlies predication, is unlikely to proceed and succeed blindly, without consciousness. This said, predicative thinking and communication can be, and often are, routinized to the point of operating effortlessly, spontaneously, and probably without conscious processing. At the same time, as noted before, we should not discount the likely possibility that spontaneous coinstantiations in normal thinking and communication parade as predications, courtesy of their regimented surface expressions in language.

There is also a more intriguing ontogenetic question: Is the development of the child's predication competence somehow intertwined with that of consciousness? Consider some of the facts discussed in earlier chapters. The predication competence is assembled by the child's mind in conditions that require intersubjective mind-to-mind, give-and-take sort of loops that convey one's mental intent and register the other's, first bilaterally and then in triangulating the world. To engage and manage such loops, extract the information conveyed in various joint ventures with adults, and intently use the loops to reach adult-assisted goals, the young child must be able to monitor and control, or self-regulate,her relatedness to the adult and the shared world in a flexible, continually adjustable manner. It is a self-regulation exercised first in perceptuomotor and affective modalities, and later in more sophisticated conative and cognitive modalities. It can be argued (though not here) that such self-regulation generates a *conscious* sense of the young child's perceptuomotor and affective relatedness to other people first, and then to a shared world, and later a conscious sense of more sophisticated conative and cognitive forms of world relatedness. This is self-consciousness, which I construe as a conscious sense—or consciousness—of the self-to-other and self-to-world relatedness in various mental modalities (Bogdan 2007, 2010).

The sense of self-to-world relatedness, generated by the very exercise of self-regulation, becomes conscious when the work of self-regulation meets certain conditions, such as intentfulness, the cross-modal integration of information, flexibility in representation, and so on. These, on my analysis, are among the conditions required by the development and, later, practice of predication. Since the infant's adaptation challenges emerge first and foremost in the domain of interpersonal relations, and later in that of adult-assisted relations to a shared world, the self-regulation that is most likely first to generate self-consciousness, in perceptuomotor and affective modalities, will be in the same interpersonal domains (Bogdan 2010).

It is therefore doubtful that the young child could journey mentally on the ontogenetic staircase to predication on automatic pilot and in a reflex manner, without evolving an interpersonal and later trilateral (child-world-adult) self-consciousness. Viewed in this light, the various ontogenetic adaptations that lead to the assembly of the competence for predication seem also to drive the development of various early forms of self-consciousness.

In short, the development of predicative thinking seems to be linked to that of self-consciousness (in the sense just outlined). In contrast, a coinstantiative sort of thinking that merely results in thematic categorizations of objects and properties, agents and actions, and so on, which are then fed into some mental and behavioral routines, is more likely to be automatic and unconscious.

Finally: Predicative-Looking Animals? Which animals, even though nonpredicative mentally, have the unmistakable look of predicators?

The answer, no doubt, is cats—the fatter and fluffier, the more predicative looking.

Notes

Chapter 2: Tales of Predication

Frege on Predication

About the second (saturated/unsaturated) axiom, David Wiggins (1984) writes: "Even if there really exists the incomplete sort of thing which Frege wants, it is still unclear how it can help to distinguish a sentence from a list to say that a sentence is unlike a list in mentioning something complete and then something incomplete. How is it that he who mentions something complete and then something incomplete thereby gets to say something?"

The point about saying is well taken. Saying is closer to predicating than merely representing. Saying has communicative and psychological implications that representing need not have. In contrast, Frege's view of predicating is about representing in a particular format.

Of the same second axiom, Davidson (1967, 304) says that it "seems to label a difficulty rather than solve it."

Quoting these criticisms, Gibson (2004, 6, 73–79) observes that the notion that the subject term refers to something complete and self-sufficient, and the predicate term to something incomplete and dependent, has a long history that goes back to Aristotle (substance versus attribute), and after Frege, to Russell and Peter Strawson (particulars versus universals). She also cites Frank Ramsey's (1925) reasonable retort that as far as predication is concerned, as a mode of saying or affirming a fact, any item named in a predication is incomplete, insofar as it needs to be related to another item. Particulars are incomplete and unsaturated without properties, and properties are incomplete and unsaturated without their particular instances.

As a finale to this discussion, it may be instructive—as a piece of intellectual history—to compare Frege's view of predication—idealized, reduced to explicit expression in a purified language, immunized against the vagaries of human psychology and communication—to the logical-empiricist view of science of the first decades of the twentieth century in the Berlin and Vienna circles (much influenced by Frege and the early work in the foundations of mathematics). The latter, too, envisaged an idealized language of science, explicitly defined in empirically intelligible terms, logically disciplined, and rigorously purified of the psychological, pragmatic, and communicational imperfections. Yet a few decades later, this pristine view of science came under increasing pressure from, and slowly yielded to the convergent impact of, the Quine-Duhem thesis on the pragmatic fluidity and coherence of scientific thinking, and the ideological, social, and psychological dimensions of scientific practice, revealed in the influential works of Thomas Kuhn, Paul Feyerabend, Russell Hanson, Imre Lakatos, and others.

I do not think the parallel should be pushed too far. But it is worth retaining that in both cases, of ordinary cognition and scientific research, the disciplined surface expression of mental contents—a mental representation or a scientific statement or even theory, respectively—should not be taken as an accurate reflection of, or reliable guide to, the actual nature and complexity of those contents, let alone the mental processes and research practices (respectively) that produce those contents.

Reification of Animal Propositions

Bermudez does not make this reification mistake, since he has an independent and astute procedure to parse animal thoughts into structural components, which are the categories of objects and properties/relations, respectively. Yet as I argued, this seems to be *all* that his analysis can claim to deliver plausibly. Nevertheless, Bermudez's gambit of using a somewhat technical predicative language to map out closely (if not isomorphically) the structural thoughts of animals may suggest the beginning of an ontological reification of animal predication. Consider the following passage: "Let us assume that we are dealing with the simplest type of [animal] thought. These are thoughts to the effect that a certain individual (relative to a particular ontology) has a certain property. In the case of an atomic thought, there will be two aspects to the canonical specification of the utility condition [a belief content], corresponding to the nominative and predicative thought-constituents" (Bermudez 2003, 107). So construed and analyzed, an atomic thought of an animal looks predicative. Yet again, the predication itself has not been demonstrated, but the canonical specification may create this impression. What is canonically specified is, at best, a thematic coinstantiation with a minimal propositional content.

Naive versus Folk Psychology

Naive psychology is (what I will call) an early ontogenetic adaptation (or rather, set of adaptations), a kind of know-how that is exercised spontaneously in registering and representing affects and emotions, gaze and attention, seeing and knowing, simple desires, intents behind actions, and so on, most often in terms of their overt expressions, whether facial, behavioral, vocal, or contextual (Bogdan 2003). It is this early naive psychology that will be shown to be most instrumental in the development of coreference, word acquisition, and predication.

I think that what philosophers call folk or commonsense psychology builds on and expands this early naive psychology by recruiting further abilities, such as inference, imagination, pretense, introspection, reflective simulation, and more, and appeals to sundry generalizations and norms, many originating in language use and cultural practices. This new gadgetry is designed to interpret the more complex and less overt states and attitudes of other minds, such as intentions, opinions, or expectations. Unlike the early naive psychology, whose basic capabilities are in place around the age of four, folk psychology appears to develop later. The early naive psychology is exercised effortlessly and uniformly by most people, whereas the exercise of folk psychology may require some mental effort and may even show some variation, depending on insight, social and cultural experience, contact with other bodies of knowledge (e.g., science, religion, and psychoanalysis), and still other factors (Bogdan 1997). I think that in their considerations about propositions and propositional attitudes, Paul Churchland, and to a large extent Sellars and Davidson, had in mind this later folk psychology rather than the early naive psychology.

These sketchy remarks do not paint the tidy and monolithic picture that is usually associated with the competence generally called theory of mind or mindeading (in addition to other names). Such a picture would be unrealistic from evolutionary and developmental perspectives. Our understanding of minds is a complex enterprise that is gradually assembled during childhood out of many disparate abilities, some with a history of natural and sexual selection, others with a history of ontogenetic selection, and still others probably selected culturally (Bogdan 1997, 2000, 2005, 2010).

Chapter 4: Roots

Mead

In 1934, George Herbert Mead was writing that

> the relationship between a given stimulus—as a gesture—and the later phases of the social act of which it is an early (if not the initial) phase constitutes the field within which meaning originates and exists. Meaning is thus a development of something objectively there as a relation between certain phases of the social act; it is not a psychical addition to that act and it is not an "idea" as traditionally conceived. A gesture by one organism, the resultant of the social act in which the gesture is an early phase, and the response of another organism to the gesture, are the relata in a triple or threefold relationship of gesture to first organism, of gesture to second organism, and of gesture to subsequent phases of the given social act; and this threefold relationship constitutes the matrix within which meaning arises. (76)

About twenty-five years earlier, Mead (1910, 132–133) suggested explicitly that "the consciousness of meaning . . . is a consciousness of one's own attitudes of response, as they answer to, control, and interpret the gestures of others." I think it would not be too far-fetched to say that Grice's analysis of meaning, read psychologically, develops and explicates this basic insight of Mead.

Besides anticipating the general thrust of Grice's view of meaning, what I find interesting about Mead's idea is that it has the historical wisdom to begin with gestures, liberally construed, which are the precursors of words both in ontogeny and most likely human phylogeny. These gestural precedents could explain why, in both historical frames, the acquisition of words does and did take place (respectively) in a relatively familiar matrix of communication of meaning—again, continuity through change. I will indulge in a few more evolutionary speculations in chapter 6.

Grice Read Developmentally

Given the tumultuous philosophical debates around Grice's account of communicative meaning, some clarifications are needed to preempt misunderstandings and tailor his account to the developmental perspective of this book. Since I begin with prelinguistic communication, the more general notion of communicator replaces that of speaker. Furthermore, we need not assume—and indeed shouldn't—that young children need a full naive psychology of attitudes to satisfy the Gricean conditions. Prelinguistic children do not recognize thoughts, beliefs, intentions, or other complex attitudes, yet they do recognize emotions and other outwardly expressed mental states through bilateral mind-to-mind interactions.

My developmental reading of Grice's account is that the young child can recognize another person's intent to express a mental state, such as emotion or attention, which is directed at the child (and later at the world), without necessarily recognizing a full intention, as is often the case in mature communication. I take this recognition of another person's intent actually to be the recognition of another person's agency, motives (in Trevarthen's sense), and effort, as they are expressed in emotions, affects, and attention—at least in the earliest bilateral stages. It is also a recognition that these mentally expressed agency, motives, and effort are directed at the child. It is in these terms that I read the two Gricean conditions.

Another point to keep in mind is that the child-adult communication by shared meaning need not require (as frequently feared) a regress of mutual recognition of mental states, such as intents—a regress that on the classical Gricean analysis, would entail increasingly higher-order metarepresentations of propositional attitudes. My position is motivated by the notion that young children do not represent propositional attitudes until after the age of three to four, and cannot handle metarepresentation and its recursion until a few years later (Perner 1991; also Bogdan 2003). Even adult communication need not involve such (limited) regress or recursion, unless normal strategies, conventions, or literal uses are violated. All that is needed in normal communication is a shared context, or shared assumptions about a context, in which what is communicated is made manifest through exchanges of communicative acts that yield a mutual recognition of what is thus shared (Sperber and Wilson 1986).

Finally, my take on the Gricean account does not distinguish between declarative and imperative forms of communication, which is as it should be, since infant communication does begin in an imperative form. This position may even fit the imperative communication of apes, if it can be established that (say) their voluntary grunts and gestures are intended to reveal some condition of the communicator (pain or pleasure) and trigger some effect in the audience, and are recognized as such by the audience.

Chapter 5: Assembly

The First Words

One can think of the first words in two ways. The first words may be those that children register and seem to comprehend before they speak. These words form a sort of receptive vocabulary, available around six to eight months (P. Bloom 2000, 35). At around twelve months children start using words, which form an active vocabulary. The latter is the vocabulary I will focus on. The earliest active vocabulary progresses from babbles to a sort of protowords whose nonreferential function is instrumental (to obtain goods and services), imperative (do this, do that), interactional (get in touch), and expressive (of likes, dislikes, and so on) (Adamson 1995, chapter 7). The referents of the first active words are vague, fuzzy, and not yet explicitly, objectively, and reliably represented (Adamson 1995; P. Bloom 2000; Bruner 1983; Akhtar and Tomasello 1998; Tomasello 2003). More than the younger child, the twelve-month-old is able to attend to an external target of interest in the knowledge that the adult is also aware of the same target. Although not yet a full triangulation based on the recognition of coreferential intent, as in shared triangulations, their joint triangulations become more tightly coordinated.

Several features of the first words confirm the social ambiance of the enterprise. New names are systematically introduced and voiced by an adult who is attending to the object named and the child. In this interactional context, the names of physical things and animals seem to be registered by children without much effort. Their (innate) naive physics and naive biology are likely to be great guides and facilitators. Things are different when it comes to the names of actions, properties, relations, and spatially discontinuous arrangements (e.g., party or game), which will become the bulk of their eventual vocabulary. The referents in this latter category are by no means obvious, nor are they sufficiently constrained by the child's available concepts or naive theories of the domains involved. The informed guess is that the child solves the problem by interpreting the mental states and communicative intents of the adults as well as other clues from interactions with adults (Akhtar and Tomasello 1998; Tomasello 2003). In the case of artifacts and cultural practices, particularly those with visually different instances—another huge portion of the vocabulary—the child is likely to guess the original purposes (P. Bloom 2000).

The evidence thus suggests that the learning of the first words that refer to visible objects and properties relies heavily on the immediate child-adult interaction through joint and shared triangulations, whereas the learning of the first words that refer to nonvisible or nonobvious items (from actions to cultural practices) seems to rely heavily on the child's naive-psychological inferences about the adult's mind or behavior. Even though many first words in both categories are acquired without adult assistance, it is fair to assume that the initial adult assistance in contexts of shared ostensive protopredications shape and constrain the child's early understanding of naming in general. As noted in the text, even when acquired in unshared contexts, new words are likely to be initially treated by the young child on the model of explicit shared naming, with a virtual adult in mind, and probably with the same mental schemes that normally represent the intent/ional comments made by adults in shared triangulations of the items named.

Joint versus Shared Attention

My terminological dissidence is motivated by the debates around and divergent readings of shared attention (for surveys, see Moore and Dunham 1995; Eilan et al. 2005).

There is (what we may call) a weak reading of shared attention that may be more aptly called joint attention (or even joint gaze, if the mental focus or intent of the partner's look is not grasped). It occurs when an individual attends to a target of perception in the knowledge that another person is attending to (or looking at) the same target. Joint attention (or gaze) is when I look at an object or event knowing that you are looking at it too, after noticing your gaze directed at it and then at me—and the same for you, from your egocentric perspective.

On the strong reading, shared attention is joint attention plus the mutually recognized knowledge that both parties know that each other is attending to the same target, and make the effort, as mental intent, to impart this knowledge to the other and have it acknowledged. Given these additional features, shared attention can also influence and direct the partner's attention. Simply put, "joint" means attending together, and "shared" (in addition) means attending in a mutually acknowledged and coordinated manner. Joint attention is a meeting of the eyes, and shared attention is also a meeting of the minds, for it involves mutually exchanged and shared mental intents and attitudes (see also Povinelli and Prince 1998).

The distinction between joint and shared attention may also explain the divergent dating found in the literature—nine versus twelve versus eighteen months. The earlier dates may actually concern joint attention, whereas the fully mentalistic, shared attention may be the one emerging later. So dated, the distinction may help explain why words begin to be acquired by shared naming in the nine- to twelve-months interval, but take off dramatically around eighteen months (Adamson 1995, chapter 7).

Finally, the distinction between joint attention (or joint gaze) and shared attention may throw some light on another debate relevant to the ontogenetic story of predication. It is a debate about whether the ability for shared attention is modular, and hence innate or acquired in some fashion. Simon Baron-Cohen (1995) has presented persuasive reasons and data for the former position. My reading of Baron-Cohen's account is that it is really about joint gaze or at best joint attention, in the sense just outlined. Autistic people can do joint gaze and probably joint attention, but have a harder time with shared attention (Hobson 1993). On this view, then, joint gaze (and possibly joint attention) may be a specialized modular mechanism, whereas shared attention looks more like a socially assembled ability—not in the sense that the child learns in experience how to do shared attention but rather in the sense that the child's mind spontaneously recruits and blends several mechanisms (ontogenetic adaptations), with diverse functions, to handle the challenges of shared attention.

References

Adamson, L. B. 1995. *Communication Development During Infancy*. Boulder, CO: Westview Press.

Akhtar, N., and M. Tomasello. 1998. Intersubjectivity in early language learning and use. In *Intersubjectivity and Emotional Communication*, ed. S. Braten. Cambridge: Cambridge University Press.

Alexander, R. 1990. How humans evolved. University of Michigan Museum of Zoology *Special Publication* 1: 1–38.

Anderson, M. L., and T. Oates. 2005. Prelinguistic agents will form only egocentric representation. *Behavioral and Brain Sciences* 26: 284–285.

Arbib, M. 2005. From monkey-like action recognition to human language. *Behavioral and Brain Sciences* 28: 105–141.

Astington, J. W., P. L. Harris, and D. Olson, eds. 1988. *Developing Theories of Mind*. Cambridge: Cambridge University Press.

Baldwin, D. A. 1993. Infants' ability to consult the speakers for clues to word reference. *Journal of Child Language* 20: 395–418.

Baldwin, D. A., and L. J. Moses. 1994. Early understanding of referential intent and attentional focus. In *Children's Early Understanding of Mind*, ed. C. Lewis and P. Mitchell. Hillsdale, NJ: Erlbaum.

Baron-Cohen, S. 1991. Precursors to a theory of mind: Understanding attention in others. In *Natural Theories of Mind*, ed. A. Whiten. Oxford: Blackwell.

Baron-Cohen, S. 1995. *Mindblindness*. Cambridge, MA: MIT Press.

Bartsch, K., and H. Wellman. 1995. *Children's Talk about the Mind*. New York: Oxford University Press.

Barwise, J., and J. Perry. 1983. *Situations and Attitudes*. Cambridge, MA: MIT Press.

Bates, E. 1976. *Language and Context*. New York: Academic Press.

Bates, E. 1979. *The Emergence of Symbols*. New York: Academic Press.

Bermudez, J. 1998. *The Paradox of Self-Consciousness*. Cambridge, MA: MIT Press

Bermudez, J. 2003. *Thoughts without Words*. Oxford: Oxford University Press.

Bickerton, D. 1990. *Language and Species*. Chicago: University of Chicago Press.

Bickerton, D. 2000. How protolanguage became language. In *The Evolutionary Emergence of Language*, ed. C. Knight, M. Studdert-Kennedy, and J. R. Hurford. Cambridge: Cambridge University Press.

Bickerton, D. 2004. Language evolution. Available at <http: //www.derekbickerton.com>.

Bjorklund, D. F. 2000. *Children's Thinking*. Pacific Grove, CA: Brooks/Cole.

Bjorklund, D. F., and A. Pellegrini. 2002. *The Origins of Human Nature*. Washington, DC: American Psychological Association.

Bloom, L. 1993. *The Transition from Infancy to Language*. Cambridge: Cambridge University Press.

Bloom, P. 2000. *How Children Learn the Meanings of Words*. Cambridge, MA: MIT Press.

Bogdan, R. J. 1983. Fodor's representations. *Cognition and Brain Theory* 6: 237–249.

Bogdan, R. J. 1987. Mind, content, and information. *Synthese* 70: 205–227.

Bogdan, R. J. 1989. Does semantics run the psyche? *Philosophy and Phenomenological Research* 49: 687–700.

Bogdan, R. J. 1993. The architectural nonchalance of commonsense psychology. *Mind and Language* 8: 189–205.

Bogdan, R. J. 1994. *Grounds for Cognition*. Hillsdale, NJ: Erlbaum.

Bogdan, R. J. 1997. *Interpreting Minds*. Cambridge, MA: MIT Press.

Bogdan, R. J. 2000. *Minding Minds*. Cambridge, MA: MIT Press.

Bogdan, R. J. 2001. Developing mental abilities by representing intentionality. *Synthese* 129: 233–258.

Bogdan, R. J. 2003. Watch your metastep: The first-order limits of early intentional attributions. In *Persons*, ed. C. Kanzian. Vienna: Holder-Pichler-Tempsky.

Bogdan, R. J. 2005. Pretending as imaginative rehearsal for cultural conformity. *Journal of Cognition and Culture* 5: 191–213.

Bogdan, R. J. 2007. Inside loops. *Synthese* 159: 235–251.

Bogdan, R. J. 2010. *Our Own Minds*. Cambridge, MA: MIT Press.

Boyd, R., and J. B. Silk. 1997. *How Humans Evolved.* New York: W. W. Norton.

Bretherton, I. 1991. Intentional communication and the development of an understanding of mind. In *Children's Theories of Mind,* ed. D. Frye and C. Moore. Hillsdale, NJ: Erlbaum.

Bruner, J. 1983. *Child's Talk.* New York: W. W. Norton.

Carey, S. 1985. *Conceptual Change in Childhood.* Cambridge, MA: MIT Press.

Carruthers, P. 2005. Distinctively human thinking. In *The Innate Mind,* ed. P. Carruthers, S. Laurence, and S. Stich. Cambridge: Cambridge University Press.

Changeux, J.-P. 1985. *The Neuronal Man.* Oxford: Oxford University Press.

Chisholm, J. S. 1988. Toward a developmental evolutionary ecology of humans. In *Sociobiological Perspectives on Human Development,* ed. K. B. MacDonald. New York: Springer-Verlag.

Churchland, P. 1979. *Scientific Realism and the Plasticity of Mind.* Cambridge: Cambridge University Press.

Clark, E., and H. Clark. 1977. *Psychology and Language.* New York: Harcourt Brace Jovanovich.

Cook Wilson, J. 1926. *Statement and Inference with Other Philosophical Papers.* Oxford: Oxford University Press.

Davidson, D. 1967. Truth and meaning. *Synthese* 17: 304–323.

Davidson, D. 1984. *Inquiries into Truth and Interpretation.* Oxford: Oxford University Press.

Davidson, D. 2001. *Subjective, Intersubjective, Objective.* Oxford: Oxford University Press.

Davidson, D. 2005. *Truth and Predication.* Cambridge, MA: Harvard University Press.

Deacon, T. 1997. *The Symbolic Species.* New York: W. W. Norton.

Dennett, D. 1991. *Consciousness Explained.* Boston: Little, Brown.

Dennett, D. 1995. *Darwin's Dangerous Idea.* Boston: Little, Brown.

Dickinson, A., and D. Shanks. 1995. Instrumental action and causal representation. In *Causal Cognition,* ed. D. Sperber, D. Premack, and A. J. Premack. Oxford: Oxford University Press.

Donald, M. 1991. *Origins of the Modern Mind.* Cambridge, MA: Harvard University Press.

Dretske, F. 1969. *Seeing and Knowing.* Chicago: University of Chicago Press.

Dretske, F. 1972. Contrastive statements. *Philosophical Review* 81: 411–437.

Dretske, F. 1989. *Explaining Behavior.* Cambridge, MA: MIT Press.

Dummett, M. 1973. *Frege.* Cambridge, MA: Harvard University Press.

Eilan, N., C. Hoerl, T. McCormack, and J. Roessler, eds. 2005. *Joint Attention.* Oxford: Oxford University Press.

Feldman, R., L. C. Mayes, and J. E. Swain. 2005. Interaction synchrony and neural circuits contribute to shared intentionality. *Behavioral and Brain Sciences* 28: 697–698.

Fodor, J. 1975. *The Language of Thought.* London: Crown.

Frege, G. 1891. Function and concept. In *Translations from the Philosophical Writings of Gottlob Frege.* New York: Philosophical Library.

Gibson, M. 2004. *From Naming to Saying.* Oxford: Blackwell.

Gomez, J. C. 1998. Do concepts of intersubjectivity apply to nonhuman primates? In *Intersubjective Communication and Emotion in Ontogeny,* ed. S. Braten. Cambridge: Cambridge University Press.

Gomez, J. C. 2005. Joint attention and the notion of subject. In *Joint Attention,* ed. N. Eilan et al. Oxford: Oxford University Press.

Gopnik, A., and A. N. Meltzoff. 1997. *Words, Thoughts, and Theories.* Cambridge, MA: MIT Press.

Greenfield, P. M., and J. H. Smith. 1976. *The Structure of Communication in Early Language Development.* New York: Academic Press.

Grice, P. 1957. Meaning. *Philosophical Review* 66: 377–388.

Harris, P. 2000. *The Work of Imagination.* Oxford: Blackwell.

Hesslow, G. 2002. Conscious thought as simulation of behavior and perception. *Trends in Cognitive Science* 6: 242–247.

Hobson, R. P. 1993. *Autism and the Development of Mind.* Hillsdale, NJ: Erlbaum.

Hurford, J. R. 2005. The neural basis of predicate-argument structure. *Behavioral and Brain Sciences* 26: 261–282.

Leavens, D., and B. Todd. 2002. The development of socially mediated visual attention in late infancy. Paper presented at the thirteenth conference on infant studies, Toronto.

Lock, A. 1980. *The Guided Reinvention of Language.* London: Academic Press.

Loftus, E. 1980. *Memory.* Reading, MA: Addison-Wesley.

Mead, G. H. 1910. Social consciousness and the consciousness of meaning. *Psychological Bulletin* 7: 397–405.

Mead, G. H. 1934. *Mind, Self, and Society*. Chicago: University of Chicago Press.

Milner, A. D., and M. A. Goodale. 1995. *The Visual Brain in Action*. Oxford: Oxford University Press.

Mithen, S. 1996. *The Prehistory of the Mind*. London: Thames and Hudson.

Moore, C., and P. J. Dunham, eds. 1995. *Joint Attention*. Hillsdale, NJ: Erlbaum.

Nelson, K. 1996. *Language in Cognitive Development*. Cambridge: Cambridge University Press.

Olson, D. 1988. On the origins of beliefs and other intentional states in children. In *Developing Theories of Mind*, ed. J. W. Astington. Cambridge: Cambridge University Press.

Olson, D. 1989. Making up your mind. *Canadian Psychology* 30: 617–627.

Olson, D. 1993. The development of representations. *Canadian Psychology* 34: 293–306.

Olson, D. 1994. *The World on Paper*. Cambridge: Cambridge University Press.

Perner, J. 1991. *Understanding the Representational Mind*. Cambridge, MA: MIT Press.

Pinker, S. and P. Bloom. 1990. Natural language and natural selection. *Behavioral and Brain Sciences* 13: 707–784.

Povinelli, D. J. 1996. Chimpanzee theory of mind? In *Theories of Theories of Mind*, ed. P. Carruthers and P. K. Smith. Cambridge: Cambridge University Press.

Povinelli, D. J., and C. Prince. 1998. When the self met other. In *Self-Awareness*, ed. M. Ferrari and R. J. Sternberg. New York: Guilford Press.

Quine, W. V. 1974. *The Roots of Reference*. LaSalle, IL: Open Court.

Ramsey, F. P. 1925. Universals. *Mind* 34: 401–417.

Reddy, V. 1991. Playing with others' expectations. In *Natural Theories of Mind*, ed. A. Whiten. Oxford: Blackwell.

Reddy, V. 2005. Before the "third element." In *Joint Attention*, ed. N. Eilan et al.. Oxford: Oxford University Press.

Rizzolatti, G., L. Fadiga, V. Gallese, and L. Fogassi. 1996. Premotor cortex and the recognition of motor actions. *Cognitive Brain Research* 3: 131–141.

Rogoff, B. 1990. *Apprenticeship in Thinking*. Oxford: Oxford University Press.

Sabbagh. M. A., and D. Baldwin, D. 2005. Understanding the role of communicative intentions in word learning. In *Joint Attention*, ed. N. Eilan et al. Oxford: Oxford University Press.

Savage-Rumbaugh, S., and R. Lewin. 1996. *Kanzi*. New York: Wiley.

Sellars, W. 1956/1963. *Science, Perception, and Reality*. London: Routledge and Kegan Paul.

Seyfarth, R. 2005. Continuities in vocal communication argue against a gestural origin of language. *Behavioral and Brain Sciences* 28: 144–145.

Sperber, D., and D. Wilson. 1986. *Relevance*. Cambridge, MA: Harvard University Press.

Sterelny, K., and J. Fitness, eds. 2003. *From Mating to Mentality*. New York: Psychology Press.

Stich, S. 1983. *From Folk Psychology to Cognitive Science*. Cambridge, MA: MIT Press.

Tomasello, M. 1999. *The Cultural Origins of Human Cognition*. Cambridge, MA: Harvard University Press.

Tomasello, M. 2003. *Constructing a Language*. Cambridge, MA: Harvard University Press.

Tomasello, M., and J. Call. 1997. *Primate Cognition*. Oxford: Oxford University Press.

Tomasello, M., M. Carpenter, J. Call, T. Behne, and H. Moll. 2005. Understanding and sharing intentions. *Behavioral and Brain Sciences* 28: 675–693.

Tooby, J., and L. Cosmides. 1992. The psychological foundations of culture. In *The Adapted Mind*, ed. J. Barkow, L. Cosmides, and J. Tooby. New York: Oxford University Press.

Trevarthen, C. 1993. The self born in intersubjectivity. In *The Perceived Self*, ed. U. Neisser. Cambridge: Cambridge University Press.

Vieru, S. 1997. *Incercari de logica*. Vol. 2. Bucharest: Paideia.

Vygotsky, L. S. 1981. The genesis of higher mental functions. In *The Concept of Activity in Soviet Psychology*, ed. J. V. Wertsch. Armonk, NY: M.E. Sharpe. (Originally published in Russian in 1929.)

Vygotsky, L. S. 1962. *Thought and Language*. Cambridge, MA: MIT Press. (Orig. pub. in Russian 1934).

Wall, Carol. 1974. *Predication: A Study of Its Development*. The Hague: Mouton.

Werner, H., and B. Kaplan. 1963. *Symbol Formation*. Hillsdale, NJ: Erlbaum.

Whiten, A., ed. 1991. *Natural Theories of Mind*. Oxford: Blackwell.

Wiggins, D. 1984. The sense and reference of predicates. *Philosophical Quarterly* 34: 311–328.

Williams, G. C. 1966. *Adaptation and Natural Selection*. Princeton, NJ: Princeton University Press.

Wolpert, D., R. Miall, and M. Kawato. 1998. Internal models of the cerebellum. *Trends in Cognitive Science* 2: 338–347.

Wray, A. 2000. Holistic utterances in protolanguage: The link from primates to humans. In *The Evolutionary Emergence of Language*, ed. C. Knight, M. Studdert-Kennedy, and J. R. Hurford. Cambridge: Cambridge University Press.

Index